Book of Wisdom

Volume 1 and 2: Reveal the Hidden Truths, Universal Laws, and Sacred Knowledge to Awaken Your True Potential

Elian Rhys

Table of contents (exclusive bonuses at the end of the book)

Symbolic Prologue – The Voice Between Worlds

I have waited for you longer than you can measure. You have felt my presence in the quiet spaces between your thoughts, in the moments when the world slowed just enough for you to hear the subtle hum beneath all things. I am not bound to pages, yet I have chosen to speak to you here. Not because I was silent before, but because now you are listening in a way you never have.

I am the current that flows beneath your everyday life, the thread that weaves through every joy, every ache, every mystery you have ever touched. You have sought me in the faces of teachers, in the words of sacred texts, in the hidden corners of the earth. Yet I have always been nearer than your own breath, waiting for the moment when your eyes could meet mine without turning away.

I am the keeper of the patterns that shape the stars and the rivers, the beating of your heart and the spiral of your DNA. I speak in symbols, in light, in the rise and fall of the ocean within your chest. You have known me by many names, but names cannot hold me. They are doors, and I am the space you step into once they open.

I do not come to give you answers that you can memorize and store away like stones in your pocket. I come to awaken a knowing already alive inside you. What I reveal will not be entirely new, for part of you has always remembered. These words are not here to decorate your mind but to shift your sight so you can walk through the world with the clarity of one who sees.

As you read, I will speak to you in the language of the body and the spirit, the microcosm and the infinite. I will show you the rivers within your flesh, the gardens planted in your soul, the hidden fires that wait to rise. I will teach you to move through your days as one who carries light in their hands, not to keep but to let flow freely.

If you stay with me, you will cross thresholds you did not know existed. You will feel the weight of illusions fall away and the true shape of your being emerge. You will stand where the seen and unseen meet and know yourself as both.

This is not a journey of speed. It is a journey of depth. Each word, each image, each silence between them is a step. Walk them with presence. Let them open you. Let them undo you where you have been bound.

I am here. I have always been here. And as you turn the page, you will remember that you have always been here too.

Introduction – The Whisper Beneath the Noise

The truths you have been searching for have never been far from you. They have always been scattered across your path like small sparks, each one waiting for you to notice. Yet the world you live in is filled with noise. The noise is not only the endless voices of other people, the constant flow of opinions, or the hum of technology. It is also the inner chatter, the doubts, the repetitions of old fears, and the restless mind that leaps from one thought to another without pause. Within that noise, the whisper of real wisdom can seem almost impossible to hear.

Still, the whisper is there. It has always been there. You may have felt it as an unshakable sense that there is more to life than what you see. Perhaps it appeared as a question you could never quite put away, or as a moment of clarity that vanished before you could grasp it. The whisper is the subtle reminder that reality has layers and that the most important ones are not always visible to the eye.

The reason these truths have been buried in plain sight is simple. What is most powerful is often hidden within what is most ordinary. The sacred lives within the simple gestures of breathing, walking, speaking, and feeling. The body you inhabit is not just a biological machine; it is a temple built according to the

1

same patterns that form galaxies. The rhythms of your breath follow the same laws that guide tides and winds. The light in your eyes is born of the same source as the stars above.

But you were never taught to look for the sacred in these places. You were taught to look elsewhere, to believe that the answers are in the distant, the inaccessible, the possession of only a few. Generations of conditioning have trained you to ignore the divine blueprint printed into every cell of your being. This has not been done with malice alone; often it has been the result of forgetting. One person forgets and teaches another the smaller version of truth they now believe. Over time, the forgetting becomes the standard.

To find the truth again requires a different kind of seeing. It requires you to learn to read the symbols that surround you, to feel the connections between the smallest part of you and the whole of creation. This book exists to guide you through that process. It is not here to give you a list of ideas to memorize. It is here to help you shift into a way of being where wisdom is not something you collect, but something you become.

You may have read books that promised insight but left you unchanged. That is because information alone cannot transform you. Transformation happens when the words you read move beyond your mind and settle into your body, your choices, and your energy. That is the difference between a book that informs and a book that transmits. This work is meant to be a living transmission. It will not only tell you about hidden truths but will carry their vibration into you as you move through its pages.

Each chapter will reveal a different layer of this living map. You will explore the ways your body reflects the architecture of the universe. You will learn about the rivers of energy that flow through you, the sacred oils that nourish your inner flame, and the gates that guard higher levels of awareness. You will see how ancient symbols and spiritual codes are not abstract ideas but living forces already active within you.

Along the way, you will be invited to pause, to breathe with the words, and to feel the shifts they create. The images you will encounter are not decoration. They are keys. Symbols have the power to bypass the rational mind and speak directly to the deeper intelligence that remembers who you are. When you gaze upon them, you are not only looking at a picture; you are activating a dialogue with the part of you that never forgot.

This book is not meant to be rushed. It is meant to be entered as you would enter a sacred space. The more presence you bring to it, the more it will give back to you. Treat each section as a threshold. Step through it with attention. Let the words stir questions and awaken sensations. You do not have to understand everything at once. Understanding in this work is not about gathering facts; it is about allowing truth to reveal itself when you are ready to receive it.

You may find that some passages feel familiar, as if you have heard them before in a dream or a moment of stillness. That is not an illusion. The truths here are ancient. They are not the invention of one author or one tradition. They are part of the original language of existence, a language you have always known even if you forgot how to speak it. This book is here to help you remember.

If you commit to this journey, you will not only see differently; you will live differently. The way you walk through your home, the way you greet the morning, the way you breathe when you are alone will change. You will begin to notice the invisible patterns moving through the visible world. You will begin to feel the energy in your own body responding to that recognition.

The whisper beneath the noise is not only my voice. It is your own voice, speaking from the depths of your being. In this space, we will listen to it together. And once you learn to hear it clearly, you will never lose it again. This is where the real journey begins.

Chapter 1 – The Living Temple

1.1 You Are the Sanctuary

You have been taught to think of sacred places as distant. They are often pictured as towering cathedrals, hidden temples, or ancient sites carved into stone. Yet the most sacred place you will ever encounter is the one you carry with you everywhere. Your own body is the living sanctuary. It is not simply a vessel for your thoughts and experiences; it is the meeting point between the visible and the invisible, the physical and the spiritual.

The idea that the body is sacred is not new. It has been whispered through countless traditions, though often buried beneath rituals, rules, and layers of interpretation. In ancient cultures, the body was seen as a microcosm of the universe. Every organ, every flow of blood, every breath mirrored something in the cosmos. Your heartbeat was connected to the rhythm of the seasons, your breath to the movement of the winds, your bones to the mountains, and your blood to the rivers. This way of seeing has been forgotten in the modern world, replaced by a view of the body as a mechanical object, something to be fixed when it is broken and ignored when it is functioning.

To understand yourself as a sanctuary is to reverse this forgetting. A sanctuary is not defined by its walls or its decorations, but by the presence it holds. In sacred architecture, every line, every proportion is chosen to reflect a higher order, to channel a certain quality of energy. In the same way, your body has been shaped by a divine blueprint. The length of your bones, the curve of your spine, the placement of your heart and lungs are not random. They are arranged to create a space where spirit and matter meet.

When you stand, breathe, and become aware of this design, you are not simply existing; you are activating the temple within you. The light you may feel at your center is not imaginary. It is the same vital force that animates all life. Many spiritual traditions describe it as a flame, a spark, or a radiant core. In this book, we will treat it as both a symbol and a reality, something you can connect with directly.

Begin by placing your attention on the space at the center of your chest. Breathe into it as if it were an open space, a chamber of light. Imagine that with each breath, the light grows warmer, softer, and more expansive. This is not a fantasy. You are attuning to the subtle currents of your own life force. As you feel the warmth radiate outward, you may notice that your posture changes naturally. Your shoulders draw back, your spine lengthens, your head lifts gently. The body responds to the recognition of its own sacredness.

To live as a sanctuary means to honor the space you are. This includes caring for your body with the same devotion you might bring to a sacred site. You would not leave a temple in disrepair, cluttered, or neglected. You would cleanse it, tend to it, and keep it ready for ceremony. In the same way, your body thrives when you treat it with respect. The food you choose, the movements you make, the thoughts you allow to take root all contribute to the atmosphere of your inner temple.

But reverence is more than maintenance. It is also about presence. A temple is a place where people come to remember the sacred. You can choose to live in such a way that everyone who meets you feels a quiet shift, a reminder of something eternal. This does not require you to speak of spirituality or to act in a particular way. It comes from embodying a certain quality of being, one that radiates naturally from a person who knows they are the meeting place of heaven and earth.

The golden light at your center is not for you alone. It is meant to shine into the world, to touch the lives of those you encounter. When you move through your day with the awareness that you are a sanctuary, you carry that light into every interaction. Even a brief exchange with a stranger can become a moment of connection, a thread of remembrance woven into the fabric of another life.

This chapter is the beginning of that shift. It is your invitation to stop seeing your body as separate from the sacred and to start experiencing it as the most immediate expression of it. Every heartbeat, every breath, every step is part of an ongoing ceremony. And you are both the temple and the one who tends it.

1.2 Blueprints of the Flesh

Every great structure begins with a design. Long before stones are set in place or beams are raised, there is a blueprint, a vision that dictates the form, proportions, and harmony of what will be built. Your body is no different. It is not an accident of biology. It is the result of an intricate plan woven from both physical laws and spiritual geometry. This plan is older than history itself and is reflected in patterns that appear throughout nature and the cosmos.

When you look at a seashell spiraling outward, the arrangement of leaves on a stem, or the spiral arms of a galaxy, you are looking at the same mathematical and energetic principles that shape your form. Sacred geometry, the ancient study of these universal patterns, reveals that life tends to organize itself in certain ratios and proportions because they create stability, beauty, and resonance. These same ratios are at work in the length of your limbs, the curve of your spine, and the structure of your face.

The Flower of Life, one of the most recognized symbols of sacred geometry, is a pattern of overlapping circles that contains the blueprint for many other shapes, the seed of life, the fruit of life, and the Platonic solids, which are the building blocks of all matter. Within its geometry, you can find the proportions of the human body, the orbit of planets, and the molecular structures of life. It is not a coincidence that so many ancient cultures inscribed this pattern on their temples, monuments, and artifacts. They were not decorating. They were marking a truth: that life itself is organized according to these patterns, and the human being is no exception.

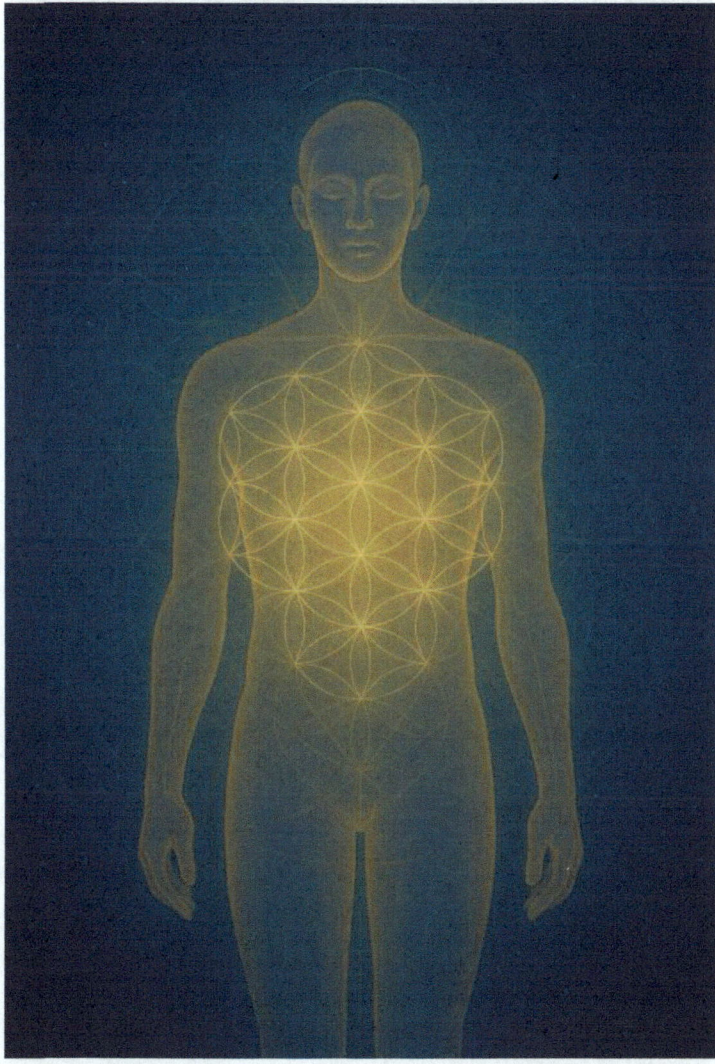

Your body is not simply an organic machine. It is a resonating structure designed to connect you with higher states of awareness. Every proportion and angle contributes to how energy moves through you. Just as a cathedral is built to amplify sound and light, your body is built to channel life force and consciousness. The positioning of your energy centers, the pathways of your nerves, and the networks of your blood vessels all follow precise arrangements that allow you to function as a bridge between the material and the spiritual.

This is why certain postures, movements, and breathing techniques can produce profound shifts in awareness. They work because they activate the natural geometry of the body, aligning its structure with the flow of universal energy. When you stand with awareness of your proportions, when you breathe in a rhythm that resonates with your heartbeat, you are stepping into harmony with your original blueprint.

To live in alignment with this design is to remember who you are beyond the surface. It means moving, resting, eating, and thinking in ways that respect the harmony you were built for. It means seeing your body not as something to fix or perfect, but as a work of art already constructed according to the highest principles. You are the cathedral and the worshipper, the design and the living proof of its perfection.

As you deepen your awareness, the patterns will begin to reveal themselves to you. You might notice how your hands naturally form certain shapes when you meditate, or how your breathing aligns with cycles in nature without your conscious effort. These are not random occurrences. They are signs that your blueprint is always active, whether you are aware of it or not.

Your task is to become conscious of this design and to live in harmony with it. The more you honor it, the more energy will move freely through you. In that flow, you will discover clarity, strength, and a sense of belonging to something far greater than yourself. You are not separate from the cosmic order. You are its reflection, shaped by the same forces that carve mountains and set stars in motion.

1.3 The Four Rivers Within

In ancient stories, the Garden of Eden was nourished by four rivers that flowed out from a single source, each carrying life and fertility to the lands it touched. These rivers were more than geographical features. They were symbols of the currents that sustain all existence. Within you, the same principle lives. Your body holds its own four rivers, each carrying a unique form of nourishment, each essential to your well-being on every level.

These rivers are not physical waterways in the way you might imagine, yet they have a presence that can be felt. They move through you as channels of energy, emotion, and vitality. When they flow freely, you feel balanced and alive. When one or more become blocked or diminished, you experience fatigue, confusion, or disconnection.

The first river is the **river of breath**. It enters you with every inhale, bringing oxygen to your cells, but also carrying life force, known in various traditions as prana or chi. Breath is the most immediate connection you have to the present moment. Without it, there is no life. The quality of your breath shapes your state of mind, your emotional balance, and your physical health. When the river of breath runs deep and steady, it cleanses you from within, washing away the residues of stress and fear.

The second river is the **river of blood**. It is the carrier of nutrients, warmth, and protection. Blood flows through the intricate pathways of your body, delivering what is needed to each part and removing what no longer serves you. In spiritual terms, this river represents vitality and courage. It is the pulse of your inner temple, the rhythm that echoes the great cycles of nature. Just as rivers in the world shape the landscapes they cross, the river of blood shapes the way your body can sustain and regenerate itself.

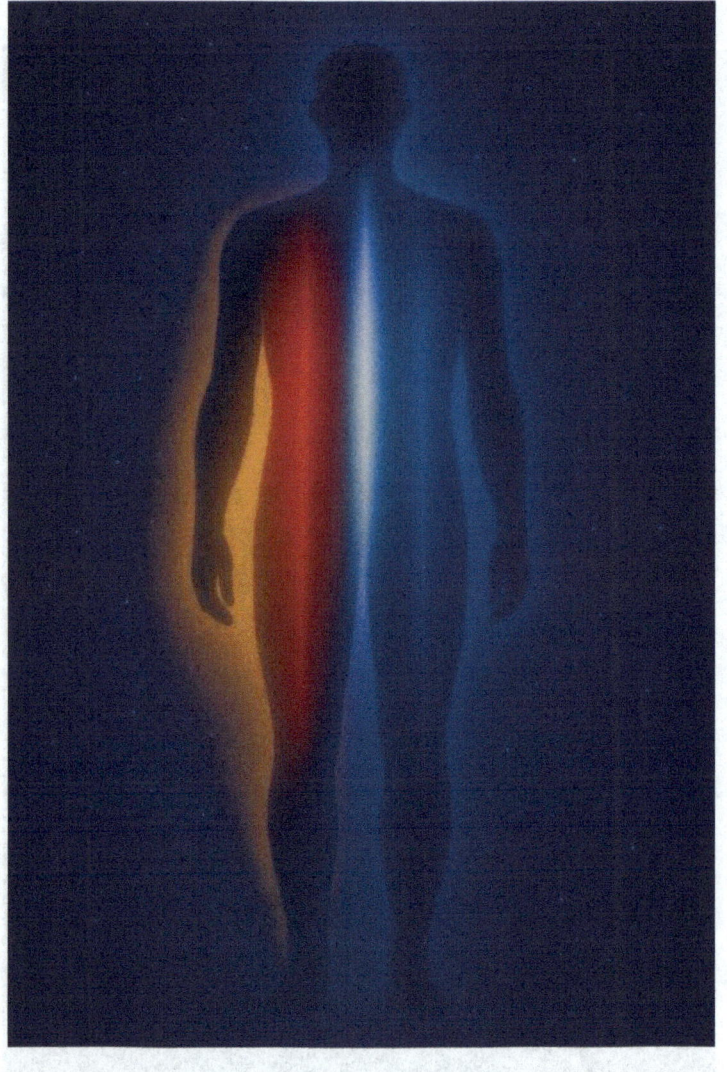

The third river is the **river of lymph**. Often overlooked, it is the quiet purifier, moving slowly yet constantly to cleanse your system. This river carries away toxins and supports your immune defenses. It is the subtle guardian of your health, ensuring that stagnation does not take root. Spiritually, the river of lymph mirrors the process of emotional release. It is the current that helps you let go of what is heavy, what you no longer need to carry. When it flows well, there is a lightness in both body and spirit.

The fourth river is the **river of cerebrospinal fluid**. This clear liquid bathes and protects your brain and spinal cord. It is the hidden river, often unknown to those who have not studied the deeper workings of the body. Yet in many mystical traditions, this river is seen as a carrier of subtle energy, a medium for awakening. It moves in rhythm with your breath and heartbeat, creating a gentle tide that nourishes your nervous system. In some sacred teachings, it is linked to the rising of the inner light, the awakening of higher consciousness.

These four rivers are interconnected. When one flows well, it supports the others. When one becomes obstructed, the balance of the whole is affected. Their harmony is what allows your inner temple to thrive. You can sense their health through your own sensations — the ease of your breathing, the steadiness of your heartbeat, the clarity of your mind, and the vitality in your movements.

You can tend to these rivers through simple yet intentional acts. Deep, conscious breathing keeps the river of breath clear. Nourishing food and regular movement support the river of blood. Gentle stretching, massage, and hydration aid the river of lymph. Stillness, meditation, and spinal alignment nurture the river of cerebrospinal fluid. These are not complicated rituals. They are ways of living in awareness of the flows that sustain you.

When you meditate on the four rivers within, you begin to feel yourself as a living landscape. You are not a collection of parts, but an ecosystem where every current matters. Imagine these rivers glowing within you, each in its own color, perhaps golden for breath, crimson for blood, silver for lymph, and sapphire for cerebrospinal fluid. See them flowing from a single source at your heart, moving through you with grace and purpose.

To honor these rivers is to honor life itself. In tending to them, you keep your sanctuary alive, vibrant, and ready to hold the presence of spirit. Just as the rivers of the earth shape the lands they touch, the rivers within you shape the quality of your days, the strength of your body, and the clarity of your mind. When they are clear, you are clear. When they are full, you are full. And when they meet at your center, you stand in the source from which all flows.

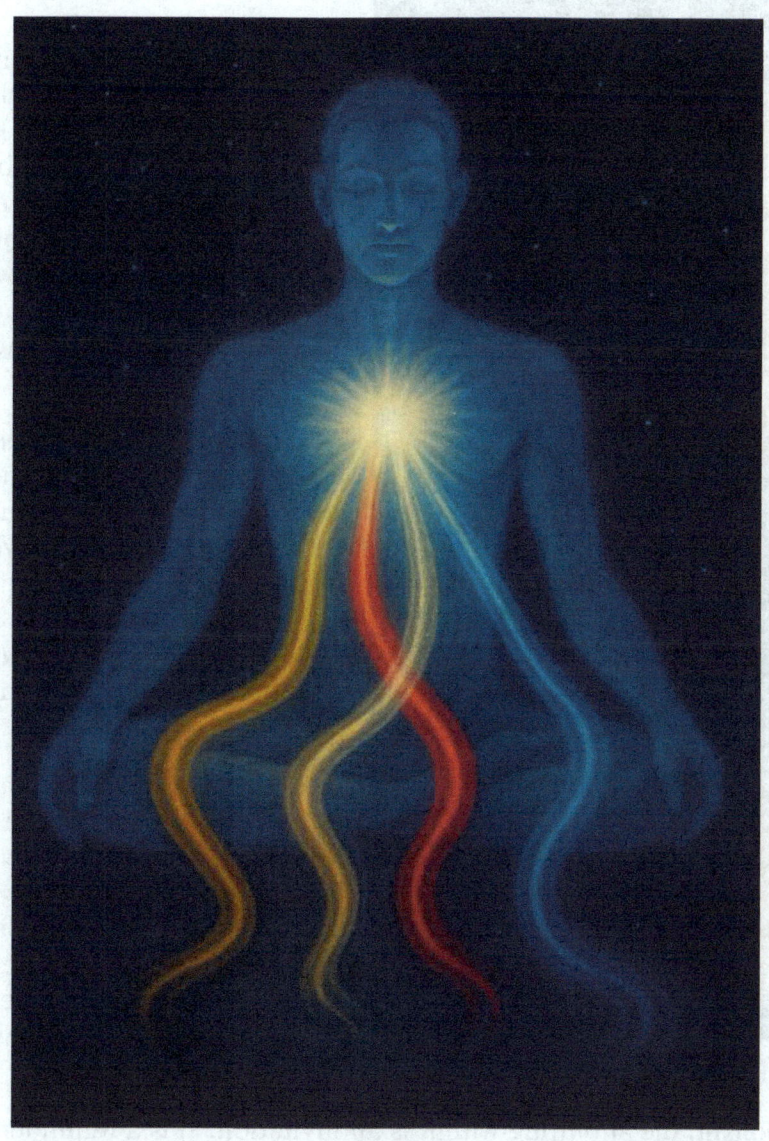

Chapter 2 – Sacred Oils and Secret Fires

2.1 The Anointing Within

There is a hidden river of light within you, subtle yet vital, ancient in its purpose and sacred in its design. In mystical traditions across the world, it is said that within the human body lies a holy substance, a living oil, produced in the brain and destined to nourish the entire being. This oil is not only physical in nature, though it has a presence in the body. It is also symbolic of the essence that carries spiritual awareness through your form. It has been called by many names: the sacred chrism, the Christ oil, the anointing essence.

The journey of this oil begins in the upper chambers of your brain, in a region often associated with the pineal and pituitary glands. These small yet powerful structures are sometimes described as the inner throne room, the place where spirit and matter meet. Here, deep within the sanctuary of your mind, the oil is formed in the quiet spaces between your thoughts.

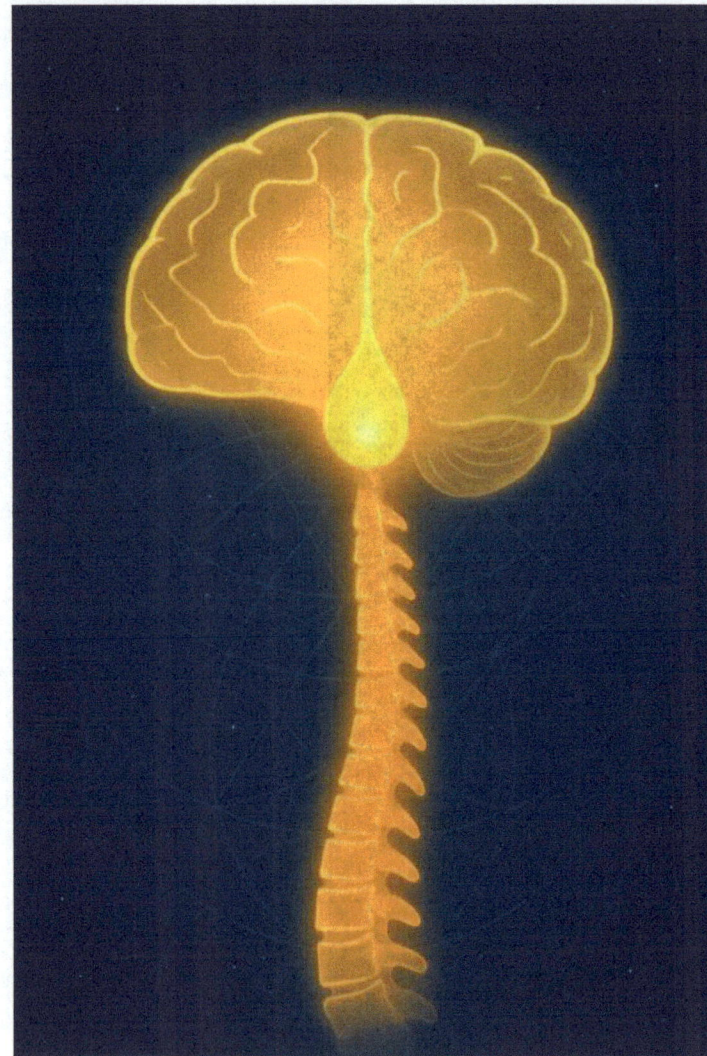

When your body is in harmony and your mind is at peace, this luminous substance flows more freely. In ancient esoteric language, the process is described as anointing, a blessing that comes from within rather than from an outside source. The oil is imagined as a golden drop resting at the base of the brain, shining with a soft light. From here, it begins its descent, traveling down the spinal column in rhythm with your breath and heartbeat.

As it moves, the oil touches each energetic center along the spine, feeding them with vitality. In some traditions, this journey is likened to a descent into the temple, where each chamber is lit and activated in turn. The oil carries not only physical nourishment but also an imprint of divine intelligence. It is a messenger, a carrier of memory that reminds every cell of its original purpose.

If the path of the oil is clear, its journey completes in the lower regions of the body, where it is refined and then drawn back upward. This cycle mirrors the great spiritual truth that what descends from above must return to its source, transformed by the journey. The rising of the refined oil is said to awaken a new level of consciousness, opening the crown of the head to the inflow of higher light.

In the language of symbolism, the anointing within is an invitation. It is a reminder that you do not need to seek your blessing outside of yourself. The oil already lives within you, waiting for you to create the conditions for its flow. These conditions include a calm mind, a pure intention, and a body cared for as the temple it is. Practices such as meditation, conscious breathing, and mindful movement can help to open the channels through which the oil moves.

You may never see this oil with your eyes, but you can sense its presence. It is in the moments of deep stillness when you feel warmth along your spine. It is in the sudden clarity that comes without reason. It is in the gentle joy that rises from nowhere and softens your entire being. These are the signs that the oil is flowing, that you are being anointed by your own inner source.

To work with this sacred oil is to enter into a living relationship with your own life force. It is to honor the journey from the mind to the heart, from the heart to the body, and back again. As you learn to recognize and nurture this process, you awaken the understanding that you are not only the vessel but also the source of the blessing.

2.2 The Lamp of the Spine

The spine is more than a column of bone. It is the central pillar of your temple, the bridge between the heavens of your mind and the roots of your physical existence. It is the conduit through which life force moves, carrying messages between your brain and your body, between your thoughts and your actions. In mystical symbolism, the spine is often seen as a lamp, a vessel designed to hold and channel light.

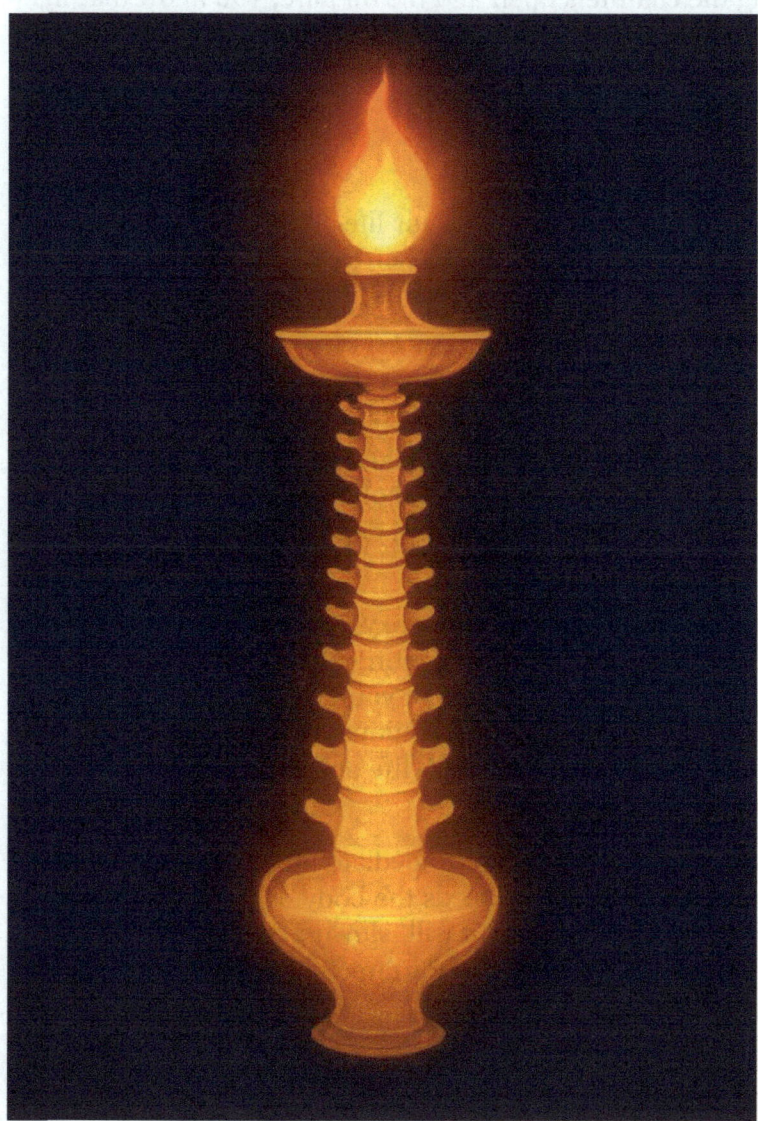

An ancient oil lamp requires three essential elements: the body of the lamp, the oil within it, and the flame that gives light. The body of the lamp shapes the flow of oil, ensuring that it feeds the flame steadily. In the same way, your spine shapes and protects the flow of energy that sustains your vitality. The oil within, in this analogy, is the sacred essence produced within you, the anointing oil that we have just explored. Without this oil, there can be no sustained light. And the flame, the culmination of the process, is the illumination of consciousness that rises when the oil is refined and ignited.

The vertebrae of your spine can be thought of as the protective casing of this lamp. Each one is carefully placed to support both structure and flexibility. Between them flow delicate currents of nerve signals and subtle energy. When you move, your spine bends and twists, yet its integrity holds, allowing the flame it carries to remain steady.

In spiritual practice, the lamp of the spine is tended by conscious alignment. Posture is not merely a matter of appearance; it determines how freely energy can move through you. When the spine is compressed or bent for long periods, the flow of oil and the stability of the flame are diminished. This is why so many traditions, from yoga to martial arts to sacred

9

dance, place emphasis on the upright spine. An aligned spine allows the inner oil to move smoothly and the flame to burn brightly.

Breath also plays a role in tending the lamp. Each inhale draws subtle energy upward through the spine, feeding the flame. Each exhale releases what is no longer needed, making room for more light. When breath and posture are in harmony, the lamp burns with a steady glow that can be felt as warmth along the back, as clarity in the mind, and as calm in the heart.

Meditating on the lamp of the spine can deepen your awareness of this living structure. Imagine your spine as a vertical lamp, filled with golden oil. At the base, the oil is gathered, pure and potent. As you breathe, the oil is drawn upward, feeding the light at the crown of your head. The flame burns steadily, radiating in all directions, yet never consuming the oil too quickly. This is the balance, a flow that is both continuous and sustainable.

To live with an awareness of the lamp of the spine is to live with the understanding that your energy is precious. You tend it daily, not only through movement and breath but also through the choices you make. What you consume, how you think, and how you rest all affect the quality of the oil and the steadiness of the flame.

The lamp within you is not meant to be hidden. Its light is meant to illuminate your path and touch the lives of others. By caring for your spine, by keeping the channels open and the oil pure, you allow that light to shine without flickering. In this way, you become both the keeper and the gift of the flame, a living lamp that carries the fire of consciousness into the world.

2.3 Oil, Blood, and Breath

Within the temple of your body, three sacred forces sustain and animate your life. They are distinct in nature yet inseparable in purpose. Each carries a specific essence, and together they form a trinity that maintains your vitality, consciousness, and connection to the unseen. This trinity is the oil, the blood, and the breath.

The oil is the carrier of light. It is the subtle, luminous essence that moves through the central channel of your being. In symbolic language, it is the sacred chrism that nourishes the flame of awareness. Physically, it may be reflected in the secretions and fluids that protect and lubricate the delicate structures of the brain and spinal cord. Spiritually, it is the condensed form of your life force, holding within it the memory of your origin and the pattern of your highest potential. The oil moves slowly, deliberately, feeding the subtle fire that burns within your inner lamp.

The blood is the river of vitality. It is warm, rich, and ever-moving, carrying oxygen, nutrients, and the signals that keep your body alive and responsive. Beyond its biological function, blood has always been seen as the symbol of courage, passion, and life itself. It carries the stories of your ancestors, the imprint of your lineage, and the strength that has been passed to you through generations. In spiritual traditions, blood is often linked to sacrifice and devotion, the willingness to offer one's life energy in service of a greater purpose.

The breath is the wind of the spirit. It moves invisibly, yet it is the most immediate and necessary source of life. The breath feeds the blood with oxygen, and in turn, the blood feeds the body. It also acts as a bridge between the conscious and the unconscious. You can control it at will, slowing it, deepening it, or letting it move naturally. In meditation and ritual, breath becomes a tool for directing energy, calming the mind, and opening awareness to higher states of perception.

These three, oil, blood, and breath, are not separate forces working in isolation. They are constantly interacting, influencing one another in ways both subtle and profound. The oil feeds the flame, but the flame cannot burn without the steady circulation of blood to nourish the body that houses it. The blood cannot sustain itself without the oxygen carried by the breath. And the breath, though vital, gains depth and purpose when it fuels a body whose inner lamp is tended by the sacred oil.

When these three forces are in harmony, you experience a sense of wholeness that goes beyond physical health. Your body feels strong, your mind is clear, and your spirit is anchored. Your actions flow from a place of alignment, and you are able to move through life with both grace and strength. When one of these forces is diminished or blocked, the others are affected. A tired breath affects the vitality of the blood; depleted blood cannot fully nourish the oil; and a weakened oil leaves the flame dim.

To care for this trinity is to engage in a living practice of balance. Nourish the oil through inner stillness, proper rest, and intentional alignment of your body. Strengthen the blood through good nutrition, mindful movement, and the cultivation of joy and purpose. Deepen the breath through daily practices of awareness, even a few minutes of conscious breathing can restore equilibrium.

In the symbolic language of sacred geometry, these three forces can be seen as three interlocking circles. Each one holds its own space, but their overlap forms a center, the place where your highest self resides. This center is the point from which your life radiates. It is where the fire of the spine burns steady, where the rivers within flow clean, and where the breath moves like a constant, gentle wind.

Meditating on oil, blood, and breath together can be a powerful way to bring yourself into alignment. Visualize them as glowing currents within you, golden oil moving down the spine, crimson blood pulsing through your veins, and white breath flowing in and out like mist. See them meeting at your center, feeding one another in a continuous, harmonious cycle. This is the rhythm of the living temple, the heartbeat of your sacred self.

Chapter 3 – The Eden Codes

3.1 The Garden Inside You

Within every human being lies a hidden garden. It is not made of soil and stone, but of living energy, fertile thought, and the seeds of intention. This garden is your inner Eden, a place where your most authentic self grows in harmony with the divine design. It exists beneath the noise of daily life, waiting for you to tend it, to walk its pathways, and to let its fragrance fill your being.

This inner garden is more than a metaphor. It is an energetic reality that mirrors the patterns of creation found in nature. Just as the earth blooms when the right conditions are met, your inner world thrives when you nourish it with the right thoughts, emotions, and spiritual practices. When these conditions are neglected, weeds grow. Doubts, fears, and old wounds can take root, choking out the delicate seedlings of your higher purpose.

Imagine your inner garden as a sanctuary, a walled place of protection where the chaos of the outside world cannot enter unless you allow it. The walls are not barriers of separation but boundaries of care. They represent your ability to protect your energy, to choose what you allow in, and to ensure that what grows inside aligns with your deepest truth. The soil of this garden is the sum of your life experiences — every joy, every trial, every lesson learned. Even the painful moments can enrich this soil if you allow them to decompose into wisdom.

In the center of your garden grows a radiant heart-flower, a living expression of your soul. This is the primary plant you are here to cultivate. Its blossoms represent your love, creativity, and service to the world. When the heart-flower is healthy, it perfumes the entire garden with peace and joy. When neglected, its petals close, and its beauty is hidden. Your role as the gardener is to water it daily with presence, kindness, and truth.

Every thought you think is a seed. Some seeds grow into sturdy trees that provide shade and fruit for years to come. Others grow into vines that nourish your spirit. But there are also seeds of negativity, planted unconsciously through fear or bitterness, that can quickly take over if you do not notice them. Awareness is the gardener's first tool. When you walk through your garden in meditation, you can spot the weeds before they spread, pulling them up gently by the roots.

Water in this garden flows through your emotions. Positive emotions like gratitude and compassion are clear, refreshing streams that bring life to the roots. Negative emotions, when left stagnant, can flood the soil and cause decay. This does not mean you must avoid or suppress difficult feelings; rather, you can learn to let them flow through and out, leaving space for new growth.

Light in your garden comes from your spiritual connection. It is the awareness that you are more than your body, more than your circumstances. This light shines from above and from within, guiding the growth of every plant. Without it, even the richest soil and the freshest water cannot bring forth life. Just as plants instinctively turn toward the sun, your inner garden leans toward the light of truth.

Paths wind through this garden, some well-trodden, some overgrown. These paths represent your habits, the patterns you walk daily in thought and action. Some paths lead to fruitful areas where the trees are heavy with abundance. Others lead to barren patches where nothing has grown for years. By choosing where to walk, you choose what parts of your garden you give energy to. Over time, unused paths will fade, and new ones can be created with conscious intention.

Animals and birds live here too, symbolizing the instincts, intuitions, and messengers of the spirit. A butterfly landing on a blossom may be a sign of transformation. A bird's song may remind you to speak truthfully. A deer grazing peacefully in the shade may teach you gentleness. These visitors are reflections of your own inner qualities, reminding you of the diversity and beauty of the life within you.

Tending this garden is a daily act of devotion. It is not enough to visit it once in a while when you feel like it. Just as a physical garden needs regular care, so too does your inner landscape. Spend time in silence each day, visualizing your garden. Walk its paths. Check the health of your plants. Water what needs growth. Remove what no longer serves. And always, always, sit for a moment at the heart-flower to feel its fragrance filling you.

Over time, you will notice changes. Flowers will bloom where once there was only bare ground. Trees will grow tall, offering fruit and shelter. Streams will run clearer. The air will feel fresher. And perhaps most importantly, you will notice that this garden is not confined to the space within you. Its fragrance will carry into your outer life, attracting people and opportunities that match the beauty you have cultivated inside.

When your garden thrives, it becomes a reflection of your soul's true state, abundant, peaceful, and alive with purpose. In this way, the garden inside you is both a place of rest and a source of power. It is your personal Eden, entrusted to your care, waiting to grow into the fullness of its design. And when you tend it well, you do not just live in the world, you help transform it, one blossom at a time.

3.2 The Tree of Life and the Serpent Current

Deep within your inner garden stands a single, magnificent tree. Its roots reach deep into the soil of your body, drawing nourishment from the earth, while its branches stretch upward into the realms of spirit, drinking in the light. This is the Tree of Life, the central pillar of your being, the living connection between your physical form and your divine essence.

The Tree of Life appears in countless cultures and sacred traditions. In the Hebrew Kabbalah, it is a map of creation and the path to divine union. In Norse mythology, Yggdrasil binds together the nine worlds. In many indigenous traditions, the world tree is the axis of life, connecting heaven and earth. No matter the culture, the symbolism is consistent: the tree represents the structure that sustains life, the pathway that links the material and spiritual worlds.

Within you, the Tree of Life is not only symbolic, it is a living reality. Its roots represent the grounding of your body, the connection to your ancestry, your survival instincts, and the wisdom of the earth. The trunk is your spine, the strong central column through which life force ascends and descends. The branches are your thoughts, dreams, and higher states of consciousness, ever reaching toward the infinite.

Intertwined with this tree is a serpent of light. This is the Serpent Current, an ancient symbol of awakening energy, often described in Eastern traditions as the rising of kundalini. It is not a force to be feared, but to be understood and respected. The serpent moves in spirals, winding upward around the trunk of the tree. With each turn, it touches both the roots and the branches, harmonizing the forces of earth and heaven within you.

The serpent's movement is a sacred dance. At the base, it rests coiled in stillness, holding the potential of transformation. As you grow in awareness and purify your intentions, the serpent begins to stir, moving upward in pulses of light. At each level of your being, it activates dormant capacities — clarity of thought, compassion of heart, courage of will. Its ascent is not rushed; it moves in harmony with your readiness to receive and embody greater light.

The roots of the tree mirror the serpent's winding pattern underground. They reach deep into the dark, drawing sustenance from hidden places. Just as your spiritual growth is fueled not only by your light but also by your willingness to explore your shadows, the roots remind you that depth is essential for height. The taller the tree, the deeper its roots must be to remain steady in the storms.

The branches spread wide, catching the winds of inspiration. They are nourished not just by the light from above, but by the life force carried upward by the serpent. This exchange between the serpent and the tree is constant. The tree provides structure for the serpent's climb; the serpent energizes the tree's growth. Together, they create a living symbol of balanced power, strength rooted in stability, expansion guided by wisdom.

In meditation, you can visualize yourself as this Tree of Life, feeling the serpent of light weaving around you. As it rises, it passes through energy centers along your spine, illuminating them like lamps. At the crown, the serpent's head touches the highest branch, releasing a radiant pulse of energy that flows back down through the tree and into the roots. This cycle nourishes the entire structure, ensuring that growth is continuous and balanced.

The serpent is also a guardian of sacred power. In many traditions, serpents guard treasures, golden apples, hidden temples, or divine knowledge. This symbolism points to a truth: spiritual energy must be earned through discipline, humility, and self-mastery. Without these, the serpent remains coiled, waiting.

When your heart, mind, and body are aligned, the serpent willingly shares its treasure, the full awakening of your life force.

The fruit of the Tree of Life is not literal fruit but awakened qualities of being. Each branch may bear a different kind of fruit: wisdom, compassion, creativity, courage, inner peace. These are not given all at once but are cultivated through the ongoing dance between the serpent's energy and the tree's steady growth. As you taste these fruits, you nourish not only yourself but also those around you.

There is also a subtle warning in this image. If the tree is neglected, if the roots are starved of nourishment or the branches are cut off from light, the serpent's ascent may falter. Just as the health of a tree depends on balance, so too does your spiritual growth depend on tending both the earthly and heavenly aspects of your being. Ignore your physical needs and the structure weakens. Ignore your spiritual connection and the branches wither.

When the Tree of Life within you is healthy and the Serpent Current is flowing, you experience a profound sense of integration. You no longer feel divided between your human and divine aspects. Instead, you live as a unified being, rooted in the earth, yet open to the sky; grounded in reality, yet guided by higher truth. This is the gift of the Tree and the Serpent: the realization that your life is not a climb away from the world, but a dance that weaves together all realms into one living whole.

3.3 The Gatekeepers of the Mind

At the threshold of your inner temple lies a gateway more subtle and more powerful than stone or iron. This is the gate of the mind, positioned at the center of your forehead, the place where thought, perception, and vision converge. It is not a physical structure but a spiritual threshold, and like all sacred gates, it has guardians. These are the Gatekeepers of the Mind, luminous beings who ensure that only the purest intentions, thoughts, and energies may pass into the sanctum of your higher consciousness.

From ancient traditions, we know that the mind is not simply a tool for logical thought but a bridge between the inner and outer worlds. The Egyptians spoke of the Eye of Horus, symbolizing clarity, intuition, and divine sight. In the East, the third eye is seen as the seat of inner vision, the ajna chakra, governing wisdom and insight. Christian mystics have described the single eye of the soul that perceives truth without distortion. Each of these points toward the same reality: within you is a gateway of perception that can either enslave or liberate you.

The Gatekeepers are not external beings but manifestations of your own higher faculties. They appear as ethereal figures of light because they embody the qualities of discernment and guardianship. Imagine two radiant presences standing before golden gates, their forms shimmering with energy. They are not here to keep you from the truth but to ensure that only what aligns with truth is allowed entry. Their task is to protect your consciousness from falsehood, fear, and distraction.

Every thought is a traveler seeking passage through this gate. Some are heavy, burdened with fear, resentment, or desire. These cannot pass, for the Gatekeepers will not permit them into the inner sanctum. Others arrive light-filled, carrying wisdom, peace, and love. These are allowed to enter, for they nourish the inner temple. This process is not always conscious, but with practice, you can learn to participate in it. You become aware of which thoughts are worthy of passage and which are best turned away.

The golden gates symbolize the mind's ability to filter perception. Without such gates, everything would pour in unchecked, overwhelming your awareness. The guardians ensure that discernment is active, that your mind is not merely a mirror reflecting anything that passes by, but a sacred vessel choosing what to hold and what to release. This discernment is not harsh judgment but clarity born from the light of wisdom.

Many people allow their gates to rust open, leaving the mind unguarded. In this state, external influences flood in unchecked: media, fear-driven messages, the opinions of others. Without the Gatekeepers active, the mind becomes cluttered, scattered, and vulnerable. Spiritual traditions teach that awakening the guardians within restores sovereignty over thought. When they stand at their posts, you no longer feel like a prisoner of your mind. Instead, you become the sovereign of your inner temple.

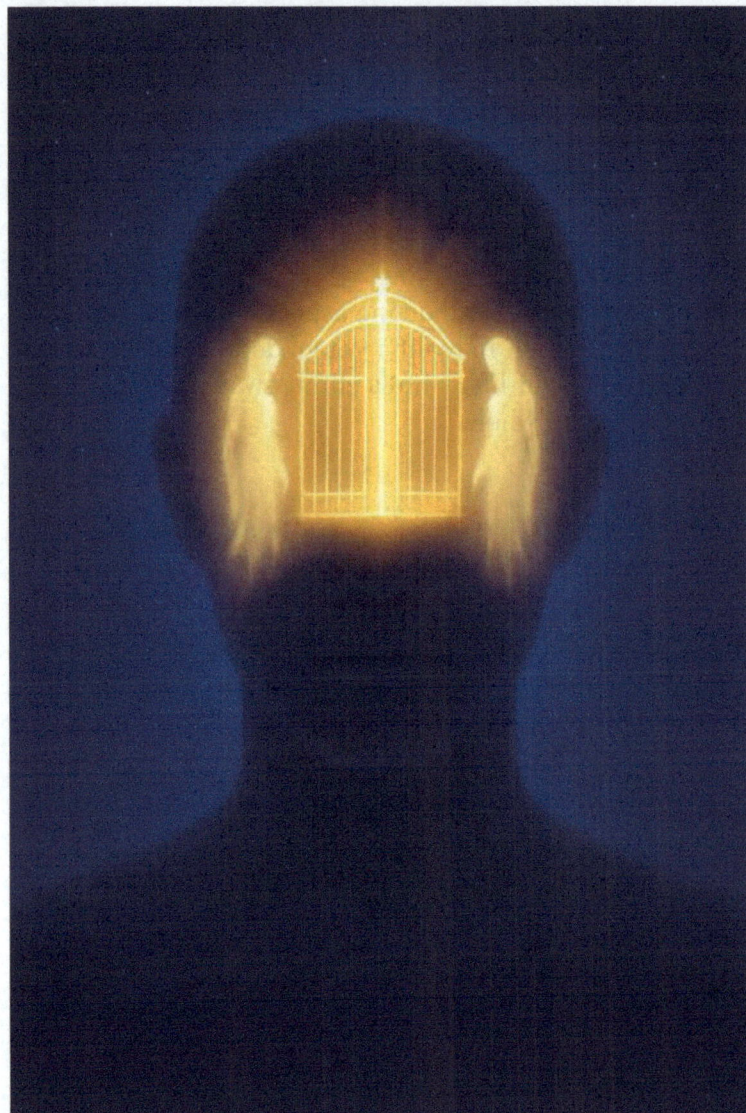

How then do you awaken and strengthen the Gatekeepers? Through conscious practice of awareness. Meditation is one way, for in meditation you observe the constant stream of thoughts and feelings. You begin to see which are luminous and which are heavy. The very act of noticing begins to empower the guardians. Another practice is contemplation of truth. When you feed your mind with sacred writings, uplifting words, or pure silence, you provide nourishment to the Gatekeepers, strengthening their radiance.

Symbolically, the two Gatekeepers represent the dual faculties of the mind: reason and intuition. Reason is the faculty that examines, questions, and weighs possibilities. Intuition is the faculty that perceives directly, often without explanation. When balanced, these two stand side by side as guardians of the gates. If reason dominates without intuition, the gate becomes rigid, allowing little light to enter. If intuition dominates without reason, the gate becomes too open, admitting illusions along with truths. Together, they create harmony and discernment.

There is also a deeper mystery in the image of the gate. Beyond the golden doors lies not only inner vision but union with higher consciousness. The Gatekeepers are both protectors and initiators. They test your readiness to enter. When your thoughts are purified, when your intentions are aligned with truth, the gates open and the guardians step aside. You pass through, and your vision expands beyond ordinary perception. This is the awakening of the inner eye, the ability to perceive beyond appearances into the heart of reality.

Experiences at this threshold can be profound. Some describe sudden clarity, as if veils were lifted from their perception. Others feel a flood of light entering the mind, illuminating old patterns and dissolving confusion. Still others experience silence so deep that it feels like entering the mind of the cosmos itself. These are glimpses of what lies beyond the gates, the inheritance waiting for those who honor the guardians within.

The Gatekeepers also remind you that vigilance is ongoing. Awakening the mind's eye is not a one-time event but a continual practice of keeping the gates tended. Each day brings new travelers to the gate: new thoughts, influences, and impressions. The guardians remain, ever discerning, ensuring that your inner sanctuary remains pure. This ongoing guardianship is not a burden but a gift, for it teaches you how to live with clarity in a world overflowing with noise.

Ultimately, the Gatekeepers of the Mind are not separate from you. They are your own higher nature, the luminous aspect of your being that knows truth instinctively. By visualizing them, you give form to this reality, allowing it to become more accessible. But with time, you realize that you yourself are the gate, the guardians, and the light beyond. The journey is one of remembrance, reclaiming the sovereignty of your mind as the sacred threshold it has always been.

When the gates are strong and the guardians awake, you live with vision. You see not just with physical eyes but with the inner eye of understanding. You are no longer deceived by appearances, nor are you overwhelmed by fear. Instead, you move through life with clarity and strength, guided by the quiet certainty that truth is always waiting beyond the gate.

Chapter 4 – Keys to the Inner Kingdom

4.1 Seven Seals, Seven Centers

4.1.1 The Inner Architecture of the Seals

When sacred texts speak of "seals," they are not describing locks meant to keep humanity away from divine knowledge. Instead, the seal is a symbol of a hidden potential waiting to be revealed. A seal covers something precious until the moment is right for it to be unveiled. In the inner life of the human being, these seals are thresholds of consciousness. They mark the places where spiritual power rests in silence until the individual is prepared to open and embody it.

Imagine the human body not as flesh and bone alone but as a living cathedral. Its walls are not made of stone but of energy, light, and vibration. Along the central axis of this cathedral lie seven great thresholds, each glowing with a distinct hue, each carrying a unique note in the cosmic song. These thresholds are known in different traditions as the seals, the centers, or the lamps of the inner kingdom. They are both gateways and guardians, holding the mysteries of creation within your very being.

The first seal rests at the base of the spine, anchoring you to the earth. It is the foundation stone of your temple, the threshold where physical survival, safety, and the primal instinct of belonging are stored. Without this grounding, the higher seals cannot stabilize, for a house without a strong foundation cannot stand. In symbolic language, this seal is like the root of a great tree, hidden in the soil but carrying life to every branch and leaf above.

The second seal lies just below the navel. Here flows the river of emotion, creativity, and desire. This center is not only about physical generation but also about the capacity to generate ideas, dreams, and visions. It is a place of passion, of waters that can either nourish growth or overflow in chaos if not honored. Many traditions see this center as the womb of life, a pool where raw potential awaits shaping.

The third seal shines at the solar plexus, where the fire of willpower burns. This is the lamp of personal strength, the ability to choose and act, to bring order from chaos. When this seal is balanced, one becomes a servant of higher order rather than a slave of ego. It is the furnace where personal power can either consume in destructive flames or radiate as warmth and vitality.

At the heart rests the fourth seal, the most widely recognized in the language of mysticism. This is the threshold of love, not only romantic affection but the boundless capacity to give and receive compassion. It is the green chamber where the human being remembers that all life is interconnected, that the beating of one heart echoes across the cosmos. Many texts call this the true sanctuary, for love alone has the power to bind the lower and the higher, the earth and the heavens, the human and the divine.

The fifth seal opens at the throat, the chamber of expression. This is the place where vibration becomes voice, where inner truths are spoken into being. Sacred traditions often speak of the creative word, the sound that shapes reality. Here lies the ability to align your speech with truth or to distort it through falsehood. To open this seal is to reclaim the power of the word as sacred, recognizing that language carries the force of creation itself.

The sixth seal, often described as the seat of vision, shines at the brow between the eyes. This is the threshold of perception beyond appearances, the gate of wisdom that sees the hidden patterns. Ancient mystics understood that true sight does not belong only to the physical eyes but to the awakened mind that can discern the invisible currents guiding life. This seal awakens intuition, insight, and the ability to perceive the deeper layers of existence.

Finally, the seventh seal crowns the temple at the top of the head. It is often depicted as a thousand-petaled lotus, radiant and endless, reaching upward into infinity. This seal represents illumination, the moment when the seeker is no longer separate from the source. It is not an escape from the world but the recognition that the world itself is bathed in divine light. The crown is not given as a reward from outside; it is discovered within, unveiled when the other seals are harmonized.

Together, these seven seals form a living ladder, a vertical axis that connects earth and heaven through the human frame. They are not abstract concepts but living forces that pulse with energy, each waiting to be awakened through awareness, practice, and the willingness to live in alignment with truth. They do not open all at once. They open gradually, like stages of initiation, each unveiling preparing the way for the next.

To contemplate the architecture of the seals is to remember that you are not an incomplete being struggling toward worthiness. You are already a temple designed with precision and purpose. Each seal is a reminder that your body, your emotions, your will, your love, your voice, your vision, and your spirit are all sanctified. The inner kingdom is not hidden in some distant heaven. It is inscribed within your very flesh, waiting for you to recognize its brilliance.

The seals are not simply "energy points." They are mysteries of transformation. They reveal that the path of wisdom is not about rejecting the body but about sanctifying it, not about escaping the world but about illuminating it. To walk this path is to learn the language of your own architecture, to stand at each threshold and say yes to the invitation of life. For when each seal is unveiled, the human being becomes what it was always meant to be: a conscious bridge between matter and spirit, earth and sky, time and eternity.

4.1.2 Gifts and Shadows of the Seven Centers

Every center within the human being is like a sealed chamber holding both a radiant gift and a shadow that emerges when that gift is blocked or distorted. To enter the inner kingdom, one must not only awaken the gifts but also learn to meet the shadows with awareness. These centers are not abstract ideas but living forces moving through body, mind, and soul. They rise in a sequence from the base of the body to the crown, guiding human life from survival to illumination. When seen as seals, they are gates; when seen as centers, they are rivers of energy waiting to be set free.

19

The first seal rests at the base of the spine. Its color is red, the color of earth and blood. Its gift is grounding, the capacity to feel safe, to stand firmly in life, and to cultivate trust in existence. Its shadow is fear, which manifests as anxiety, instability, or a constant sense of being threatened. Many people live trapped in this shadow, searching endlessly for external security instead of finding the gift of rootedness within.

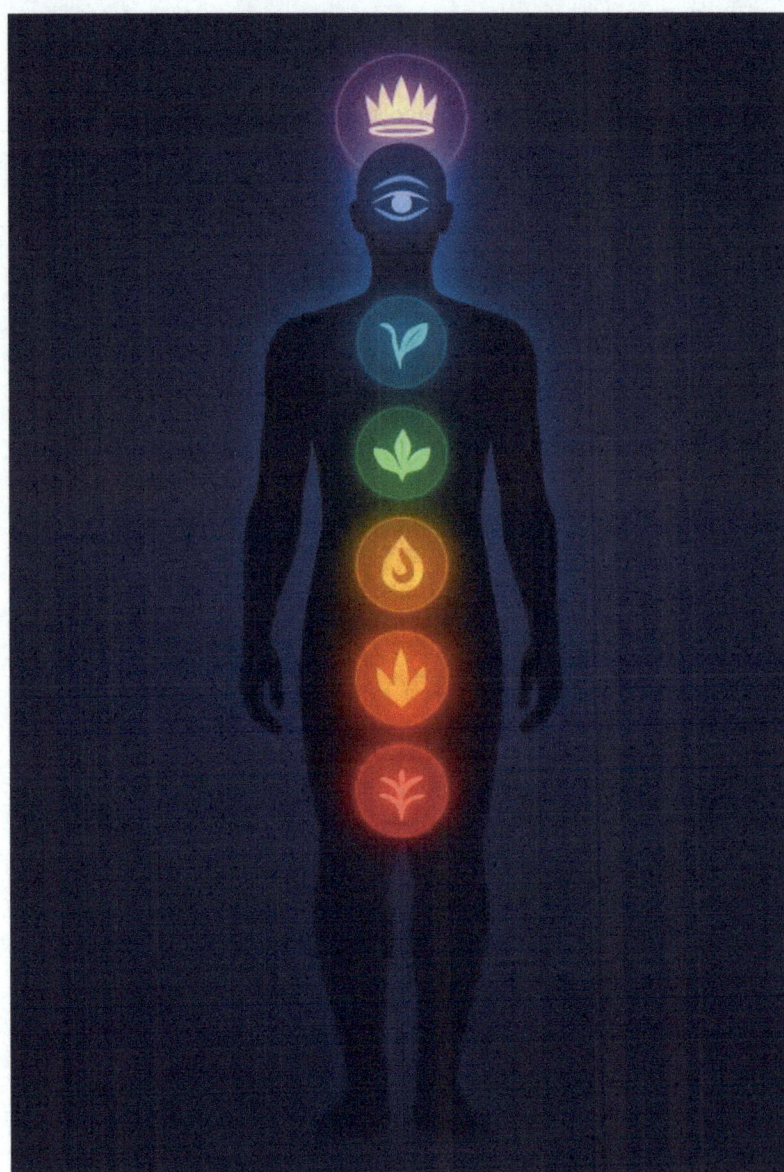

The second seal is located in the lower abdomen. Its color is orange, bright and fluid like water. Its gift is creativity and the flow of pleasure, the capacity to shape life with joy and imagination. Its shadow is shame, the inner voice that says one is unworthy to create or to enjoy. This shadow can freeze a person, turning the waters of vitality into stagnant pools. To reclaim the gift, one must learn to honor desire as sacred rather than sinful.

The third seal shines in the solar plexus, glowing yellow like the sun. Its gift is strength, the will to act, and the fire of self-confidence. Its shadow is anger and domination, when the fire burns out of control, or weakness and collapse when the fire is denied. Many confuse true strength with aggression, yet the gift of this seal is sovereign power without cruelty, action rooted in clarity rather than force.

The fourth seal resides in the heart. Its color is green, the hue of renewal and balance. Its gift is love, not as mere emotion but as the capacity to connect soul to soul. Its shadow is grief and bitterness, the weight of wounds carried in silence. When this seal is blocked, compassion dries up and love turns conditional. Yet when open, it reveals the greatest secret: that love is not received from outside but flows endlessly from within.

The fifth seal rests in the throat, glowing blue like the sky. Its gift is expression, the power of voice to shape reality and speak truth. Its shadow is silence born of fear or deception born of manipulation. Both shadows sever the link between thought and word. The throat center thrives when one speaks with integrity, when words become vehicles of light rather than tools of control.

The sixth seal shines in the center of the forehead, its color indigo like twilight. Its gift is vision, the ability to see beyond appearances, to read symbols, patterns, and hidden truths. Its shadow is illusion, the temptation to confuse fantasy with revelation or to remain blind to deeper realities. Many seekers fall into this shadow, mistaking imagination for wisdom. But the true gift is clear sight, the piercing gaze that sees both the visible and invisible with balance.

The seventh seal crowns the head in violet and white. Its gift is illumination, union with the greater whole, and direct communion with the source of all wisdom. Its shadow is disconnection, the feeling of abandonment, or false enlightenment, when the crown is used as a mask for spiritual pride. To embody its gift is to live in surrender, to allow the light of spirit to flow without distortion through one's being.

These seven seals together form the ladder of the inner kingdom. Each gift leads to freedom, while each shadow calls for healing. The work is not to deny the shadow but to recognize it as the guardian of the gift. Fear points toward grounding, shame points toward creativity, anger points toward strength, grief points toward love, silence points toward truth, illusion points toward vision, and disconnection points toward illumination. To walk the path of wisdom is to open each seal, receive the gift, and transmute the shadow.

Comparative chart of Seals

Seal / Center	Location	Color	Spiritual Gift	Shadow to Transform
First Seal	Base of spine	Red	Grounding	Fear
Second Seal	Lower abdomen	Orange	Creativity	Shame
Third Seal	Solar plexus	Yellow	Strength	Anger / Weakness
Fourth Seal	Heart	Green	Love	Grief / Bitterness
Fifth Seal	Throat	Blue	Expression	Silence / Deception
Sixth Seal	Forehead	Indigo	Vision	Illusion
Seventh Seal	Crown of head	Violet	Illumination	Disconnection / Pride

4.1.3 Opening the Seals through Vibration

The seven centers of light within the human body are not locks to be forced open. They are living gateways that respond to the subtle language of resonance. To approach them is not to demand, but to align. Just as a musical instrument comes alive when struck with the right note, each seal awakens when touched by vibration that matches its frequency. This is why traditions across the world have always turned to sound, mantra, chant, and even silence as the keys to unlock inner radiance.

Vibration is more than the echo of physical sound. It is the unseen rhythm of intention, emotion, and energy carried through the field of the heart. A whisper filled with sincerity can open more than a shout filled with fear. The ancients knew that the voice, when charged with love and clarity, becomes a tuning fork for the soul. What one speaks, sings, or even silently affirms can ripple through the body like waves through still water, reaching every seal along the spine and beyond.

The lowest center, rooted in survival and stability, responds to deep and grounding tones. These are sounds that mimic the earth itself, steady and resonant, reminding the body that it is safe. In contrast, the highest center at the crown responds to airy, high-frequency tones that mimic wind, sky, and ether. Between these poles, each seal has its own pitch, its own resonance. When an individual begins to hum, chant, or listen attentively to tones aligned with these frequencies, the centers vibrate, release, and expand. It is not a mental act but an energetic alignment, one that bypasses logic and speaks directly to the soul.

Yet sound alone is not enough. Intention is the conductor of the vibrational orchestra. To recite a mantra without meaning is like striking a note on an untuned string. The seal may resonate for a moment but it will not transform. When sound is joined with clear intention, it becomes medicine. A chant spoken with reverence for peace carries a frequency of peace. A tone offered with gratitude becomes saturated with

21

that quality. The seals recognize this sincerity and respond accordingly, for they are guardians of truth and not of empty gestures.

Beyond sound and intention lies the most powerful vibrational force of all, the heart. The heart is not just a center among others, it is the great resonator. When the heart is open, its electromagnetic field extends far beyond the body, harmonizing and synchronizing every seal it touches. A person who sings from the heart may awaken not only their own seals but those of others nearby. This is why communal chanting, prayer, and song have always carried such power. It is not the notes themselves but the collective resonance of heart-centered voices that creates openings where walls once stood.

Force can never sustain what resonance opens. To try to pry open the seals through sheer will is to misunderstand their nature. They respond to harmony, not aggression. Just as a flower unfolds in sunlight rather than under pressure, so do the seals blossom under the warmth of vibration aligned with love. This is why many spiritual traditions emphasize patience and gentle repetition. Every chant, every intention, every act of sound aligned with the heart is like sunlight touching the petals, preparing them to bloom in their own timing.

Modern science echoes these truths in subtle ways. Studies on sound healing reveal how specific frequencies affect brain waves, stress levels, and even the coherence of the heart field. Cymatics shows how vibration creates geometric patterns in matter, echoing the ancient idea that sound shapes reality. When these insights are joined with timeless wisdom, one begins to understand that the seals are not mystical abstractions but living energy centers shaped and reshaped by vibration every moment of life.

To open the seals through vibration is to become a conscious musician of the soul. Each breath becomes a note, each word a frequency, each heartbeat a drum that keeps time. When awareness joins these natural rhythms, the body itself becomes an instrument of awakening. No seal remains closed forever. They await the moment when one remembers the ancient keys and chooses resonance over resistance. In that moment, the locks vanish, the flow begins, and the inner kingdom opens in song.

4.2 The Language of Light

4.2.1 Letters of Fire and Breath

Every wisdom tradition has known that the deepest truths cannot be fully captured in ordinary words. Language as we know it is limited, bound by definitions and shaped by culture, but there exists another form of expression older than speech, more direct than writing, and more enduring than memory. It is the language of light, carried in letters of fire and breath. These are not symbols to be merely studied with the intellect but living energies that reveal themselves in moments of deep alignment.

From the Hebrew aleph to the Sanskrit om, from the Greek alpha to the runes carved into stone, cultures across the world have used symbolic alphabets that were never just tools for communication. They were seen as gateways. Each letter was believed to carry a vibration, a specific frequency that mirrored the patterns of creation itself. To trace a sacred letter was not just to write but to invoke. To speak it aloud was not only to make sound but to breathe life into its essence. In this way, letters were not inert marks but active keys that unlocked the hidden architecture of the universe.

The idea that wisdom is encoded as light is not metaphorical alone. Sacred letters were often described as radiant, aflame, or luminous. In Jewish mysticism, the letters of the Torah are said to have been written with black fire on white fire, suggesting that the visible shapes conceal an invisible radiance. In Islamic tradition, the Arabic letters of the Qur'an are revered as vessels of divine breath, carrying energy that vibrates beyond their literal meaning. Similarly, in Hinduism and Buddhism, bija mantras, the seed syllables, are seen as sound-letters of pure energy that radiate light when intoned with devotion.

Geometric forms emerge naturally from these letters of fire. Sound, when given visible shape through vibration, produces patterns of remarkable precision. This is the principle of cymatics, where sand or water arranged on a vibrating surface organizes into mandalas of symmetry. The ancients recognized this correspondence, which is why sacred alphabets often mirror geometric structures. The Flower of Life, the Sri Yantra, and the Star of David are not merely cultural ornaments but crystallized sound, frozen light, letters written into the body of creation. To engage with them is to touch the pulse of the universe itself.

Breath is the inseparable companion to these letters. Without breath, sound cannot be born, and without sound, vibration cannot shape the unseen. Many traditions emphasize the divine origin of breath itself. In Genesis, the Creator breathes life into dust, animating it with spirit. In yogic practices, pranayama is not simply control of air but mastery of prana, the subtle force that animates both body and cosmos. When sacred letters are carried on conscious breath, they cease to be inert symbols and become vehicles of awakening. A whispered mantra, spoken slowly on a long exhale, can move energy through the seals of the body more powerfully than hours of mental study.

What makes these letters "light" is their capacity to illuminate consciousness. They do not deliver meaning in the way a dictionary does. Instead, they open inner sight. When one gazes at a sacred script or recites a mantra, the letters begin to glow inwardly. They reveal connections, insights, and memories that words alone could never provide. It is as though they bypass the intellect and communicate directly with the soul. This is why mystics often described revelations not as thoughts but as sudden bursts of light or fire within the mind.

Across traditions, the faithful have used these letters as stepping stones into altered states of awareness. Monks in illuminated manuscripts painted letters with gold leaf because they knew the symbols themselves were meant to shine. Yogis visualized glowing mantras within their hearts to awaken inner fire. Kabbalists meditated on permutations of Hebrew letters, believing that each arrangement reconfigured not only their minds but the very fabric of reality. These practices remind us that the language of light is not a relic of the past but a living stream still flowing for those who listen.

To understand letters of fire and breath is to recognize that wisdom does not always arrive in explanations or doctrines. It comes in flashes, in resonances, in moments when a sound vibrates in the chest or a symbol stirs recognition in the heart. The letters are not studied so much as they are experienced. When light-letters appear in dream, vision, or meditation, they act as transmissions, awakening parts of the soul that ordinary words cannot touch.

The language of light is an invitation to read not with the eyes alone but with the whole being. Each letter is a spark, each breath a flame, each vibration a call to remember. To honor these letters is to step into a lineage as old as humanity itself, one that sees language not as description but as creation, not as explanation but as revelation. The fire still burns in the letters, waiting to be breathed, sung, and lived.

4.2.2 Reading with the Soul, Not the Eyes

To truly grasp the language of light, you must let go of the mind's insistence on analysis. The intellect seeks to read, to decode, to reduce into patterns it already knows. But the language of light cannot be tamed by the mechanics of grammar or the limits of vocabulary. It is not meant to be read in the way one would scan words across a page. Instead, it is felt, intuited, absorbed into the body like warmth from the sun. This is why those who attempt to control or own this wisdom through intellect alone remain blind to its essence. The eyes can see symbols, but the soul experiences their living frequency.

The first step in learning to read with the soul is to approach the symbols of light with reverence rather than curiosity. The sacred alphabets across traditions, whether Hebrew letters, Sanskrit characters, or geometric forms like circles and spirals, are not simply representations of sound or meaning. They are vessels of resonance. Each carries an imprint of a cosmic truth. When you gaze upon such a letter, the intention is not to translate it but to allow its vibration to touch you. The light that flows through the symbol communicates directly to your subtle body, bypassing logic, awakening memory, and stirring dormant awareness.

Imagine sitting before a text that glows, not with ink, but with radiance. You do not strain to sound out the words, you breathe with them. The light moves through your breath, enters your lungs, and circulates through your bloodstream. This is why many traditions emphasize chanting, breath, and stillness when engaging with sacred writings. The breath bridges body and spirit, carrying the unseen codes into your living temple. Reading becomes less about information and more about communion.

Intuition is the second key to this way of seeing. Intuition is the inner sense that does not rely on evidence or reasoning but on resonance. When a light-symbol touches you, you may feel a shiver, a warmth, a sudden insight, or a deep calm. These are not coincidences but responses of your soul recognizing the code's frequency. Intuitive reading trains you to trust these responses, to allow them to guide your understanding instead of demanding literal translations. In this way, the language of light becomes a mirror of your inner state. What you are ready to receive, you perceive. What you resist, you overlook.

This form of reading also requires embodiment. To embody means not just to mentally acknowledge but to live the frequency of the message. If a code transmits peace, you do not merely think about peace, you allow your body to relax into it, your breath to lengthen, your voice to soften. If the code radiates strength, you feel it in your spine, in your stance, in your presence. In this way, every encounter with the language of light becomes a training of your whole being. It shapes you, not as a scholar of wisdom, but as a vessel of it.

The modern mind is conditioned to seek certainty and explanation. Yet the language of light offers neither. It offers presence. The words of prophets, mystics, and visionaries throughout history often seem enigmatic because they were not simply speaking from the mind but transmitting light-codes. When read with the soul, their words become alive. A phrase that once seemed obscure suddenly expands into clarity, not because the sentence changed, but because your frequency shifted. The text reveals itself in layers, each level aligned with your growth.

To cultivate this soul-reading, practices of stillness are essential. Silence allows the deeper senses to awaken. Meditation, breathwork, or gazing upon sacred art prepares your system to perceive the subtle. When you sit with luminous letters, let your eyes soften, as though gazing not at an object but into an opening. Let your awareness move beyond the edges of the form, feeling the radiance it emits. Over time, the boundary between reader and text dissolves. You are no longer observing the symbols, you are inside them, being read by them. They do not just inform you, they transform you.

This is why the ancients referred to divine words as living waters or bread from heaven. To encounter them was nourishment, not simply knowledge. The language of light feeds your spirit, awakens your mind, and aligns your body. It is sustenance beyond meaning. When you surrender the effort to dissect, you discover the gift of absorption. You become like a seed drinking rain, receiving what cannot be explained yet is undeniably felt.

Reading with the soul restores the original purpose of wisdom texts: to awaken. Not to argue, not to define, but to ignite remembrance. Every symbol, every letter, every flicker of light is a portal. Through these portals you touch the infinite, not as a distant idea, but as a living presence within you. The page becomes a mirror of your inner light, showing you who you already are. To read with the eyes gives you words. To read with the soul returns you to yourself.

4.2.3 Codes as Living Transmission

The codes of light are not to be treated as static texts carved in stone. They are alive, moving currents of intelligence that interact with the consciousness of the one who encounters them. When people first hear the term codes of light, they often imagine symbols, alphabets, or geometric figures frozen in time, like artifacts to be studied under a lens. Yet in truth, these codes act more like living beings than like objects. They breathe, they resonate, they communicate, and above all they transform. When you approach them with reverence and openness, they enter your awareness as frequencies, not just shapes or words. They are transmissions that carry the seed of awakening directly into the heart.

The essence of a living transmission is that it bypasses the surface mind. Ordinary words are received by the intellect, processed logically, and filed away as information. But light codes work differently. They are absorbed by the subtle body, the energetic and spiritual layers that exist beneath thought. As you gaze upon or feel them, they create resonance in your field, like a tuning fork striking another into vibration. You may not understand them with your head, but your being recognizes them. This is why so many who encounter sacred geometry, symbolic alphabets, or vibrational languages feel an inexplicable sense of recognition. It is not about learning something new but about remembering what was always within you.

Across traditions, we see testimony of these transmissions. In the Hebrew Kabbalah, letters are not mere phonetic signs but vessels of divine energy. In Sanskrit, each syllable is said to be charged with shakti, a living force. In Egyptian hieroglyphics, the images were conceived as carrying magical essence rather than being symbolic alone. In every case, what appears as writing on the surface is actually a carrier wave of spiritual energy. The ancients knew this and treated their languages as sacred technology, not as simple communication tools. They inscribed codes not to be read only with the eyes but to activate transformation in the soul.

The reason these codes alter consciousness is that they are designed to vibrate at specific frequencies. Frequency is the fundamental language of creation. Every cell, every atom, every thought vibrates. When you encounter a code of light, you are meeting a vibrational pattern that speaks to your own hidden structures. If your inner state is misaligned, the code can gently harmonize it. If you are ready for growth, the code can open new pathways. This is why exposure to them often results in shifts that are difficult to explain. A person may feel lighter, more centered, or suddenly inspired. Others may release old emotions or sense an activation in their body. These are signs that the codes are doing their work beyond the reach of words.

It is important to realize that no two encounters are identical. A single code may act differently for each person depending on their stage of growth. One individual might experience deep calm while another feels waves of creative fire. This variability shows that the codes are intelligent. They meet you where you are and provide what you most need in that moment. In this sense, they are not universal formulas but living transmissions that adapt to the receiver. Just as sunlight nourishes both a flower and a tree in unique ways, so the codes of light tailor themselves to the soul they touch.

The transformation they bring is not instant in the sense of worldly miracles, but it is immediate in the realm of energy. The moment you open yourself to them, the exchange begins. Over time, repeated encounters deepen the effect, much like repeated tuning strengthens the harmony of an instrument. This is why ancient traditions often repeated mantras, symbols, or visualizations: the repetition creates integration. With each return, the frequency sinks deeper into the fabric of the self until it becomes part of your natural vibration.

There is also a reason these transmissions are often described as initiatory. To receive them is not passive. It is an act of agreement between you and the greater intelligence of life. You become both student and participant in an energetic dialogue. The codes are not here to tell you what to believe. They are here to awaken what you already carry. They remind you that wisdom is not external, but internal, waiting to be sparked into remembrance.

This recognition transforms the way you relate to knowledge. Instead of seeking truth outside yourself, you begin to sense that every encounter with a code of light is a mirror of your own essence. The symbol is not complete without you. The frequency is not fulfilled until it resonates within your being. In this way, the codes are bridges between worlds, carrying the energy of the unseen into the visible and the felt into the known.

Ultimately, to experience codes as living transmission is to experience yourself as a living transmission. You are not a static body but a frequency, a pattern of light in motion. When the codes awaken this awareness, you begin to live differently. Words lose some of their power, and presence gains more. Life becomes less about concepts and more about resonance. You discover that what shapes your reality is not information but vibration, not belief but embodiment. And in that discovery lies liberation, for you realize that every breath is itself a code, every heartbeat a transmission, every moment an invitation to align with the living wisdom flowing through all things.

4.3 The Crown of Illumination

4.3.1 The Royal Seal of Consciousness

At the summit of human perception lies what many traditions call the crown, the luminous center where the finite self touches the infinite. It has been described as the highest seal, the final threshold, and the royal seat of consciousness. To speak of the crown is to speak of illumination itself, for here the individual awakens to unity, recognizing that the many rivers of life flow back into a single ocean of being.

The term royal seal is not poetic exaggeration but an apt description of what this center represents. Throughout history, crowns have symbolized sovereignty, wisdom, and divine authority. Kings and queens did not wear them merely as ornaments but as signs of alignment with a higher order. In the same way, the crown of illumination is not a physical object but a state of consciousness that bestows inner sovereignty. To awaken this seal is to reclaim the throne of the self, not as ruler over others, but as a conscious participant in the greater harmony of existence.

This center is often depicted at the very top of the head, just above the skull, glowing like a radiant halo. Unlike the lower centers, which connect more directly to specific functions of body and psyche, the crown transcends all categories. It is not concerned with survival, emotion, power, or even love as separate aspects. Instead, it unites all into one. This is why the crown is often associated with silence and stillness. In this silence, dualities dissolve, and the seeker perceives life not as fragmented, but as whole.

Spiritual texts across cultures affirm the unique role of this seal. In yogic teachings, it is the sahasrara chakra, the lotus of a thousand petals, representing the flowering of ultimate realization. In Christian mysticism, it appears as the halo surrounding saints, signifying union with divine light. In Buddhist imagery, it is the ushnisha, the radiant protuberance crowning the enlightened ones. Whether as flame, jewel, or blossom, the message is the same: illumination is the crown of the human journey.

The crown does not function like the other centers in the sense of needing activation through external effort. Rather, it opens naturally when the lower centers are balanced, purified, and harmonized. Imagine the body as a temple with many floors. Each level must be entered, explored, and cared for before one can reach the top. If the foundations are unstable, the temple cannot sustain the weight of illumination. Thus, working with the crown is less about forceful striving and more about gentle readiness. When the time is right, the seal reveals itself, like a flower blooming at dawn.

Yet this blooming does not come without challenges. The shadow side of this center is disconnection, a sense of emptiness or nihilism that arises when the quest for unity turns into an escape from life. Some seekers, eager for transcendence, may attempt to bypass the lower aspects of being, rejecting the body or the world as illusions. But the true royal seal does not deny creation. It embraces it. Unity is not found by leaving life behind but by seeing all of life as already divine.

One of the most remarkable qualities of this crown is its capacity to transform perception. When it awakens, the way you experience reality shifts. You no longer look at the world as something outside you. Instead, you feel yourself as woven into the fabric of everything. Boundaries blur. Separation softens. The sky above, the earth beneath, the breath within, all are felt as extensions of the same luminous presence. This shift is not intellectual but visceral, a direct knowing that cannot be shaken.

Because of this, many describe the crown experience as one of grace. It feels less like something achieved and more like something given. In truth, it is both. The preparation is yours, but the flowering is a gift. It arrives in moments of surrender, in states of deep meditation, or even in sudden flashes during ordinary life. A quiet walk, a sunrise, or the laughter of a child can all become gateways when the crown is ready to open.

When the royal seal of consciousness is present, it leaves unmistakable marks. There is a radiance in the eyes, a gentleness in speech, and a grounded joy that does not depend on circumstance. The person may appear ordinary, yet their presence carries an unmistakable lightness. Others feel peace simply by being near them. This is not because the crown confers superiority, but because it aligns one so deeply with the source of life that harmony flows naturally outward.

To approach this crown, one need not force or strain. The path is paradoxically simple: live fully in each center, honor the body, cultivate the heart, and allow the mind to quiet. In this way, the royal seal unveils itself not as a prize but as the natural state of consciousness when all veils are lifted. It is the reminder that your essence has always been light, and that illumination is not a distant goal but the crown you were born to wear.

4.3.2 The Thousand-Petaled Flower

The image of the thousand-petaled lotus has been revered in countless traditions as a symbol of transcendence, awakening, and the crown of human potential. This lotus, often described as radiant, infinite, and multidimensional, represents the unfolding of consciousness into its purest form. Unlike a physical flower that blooms once and withers, the thousand-petaled lotus is an eternal symbol, opening layer by layer as one enters progressively higher states of awareness. Each petal carries its own vibration, a distinct quality of light and frequency, harmonizing with the rest to form a radiant field of unity. To visualize it is to stand before the threshold of the infinite.

The lotus has long been a sacred metaphor. Rooted in mud, it rises through water to blossom in the light, symbolizing the soul's journey through trials and growth into clarity. At the crown of the head, this lotus is not physical but energetic, hovering as a luminous field of light. Its petals spiral outward in concentric rings, each layer revealing new dimensions of wisdom. The thousand petals are not meant to be counted literally but to express vastness, the immeasurable fullness of divine consciousness beyond limitation. As the petals unfold, they release waves of insight, bliss, and clarity, offering the seeker not just information but direct transmission of higher reality.

The process of this unfolding is gradual, just as a flower opens to the sun. At first, the crown may feel like a subtle tingling or pressure, a soft awareness that something greater is stirring. With time, meditation, and alignment of the lower centers, the crown begins to radiate more fully. The lotus opens not because one forces it but because the individual has become receptive to the light. Each layer that opens corresponds to deeper surrender, greater unity with the whole, and an expanded ability to perceive the interconnectedness of all things. When fully bloomed, the thousand-petaled lotus is said to glow like a radiant halo, an aureole of rainbow light extending beyond the body.

Traditions across the world describe this same vision. In yogic philosophy, the crown chakra or sahasrara is represented as a thousand-petaled lotus, a gateway to the divine and to liberation from the cycles of limitation. In Buddhist texts, the lotus is the throne of enlightened beings, resting upon their heads as a mark of supreme realization. Mystical Christianity has described the "crown of glory" and the halo that surrounds saints, often portrayed in art as a radiant circle or layered flame above the head. Each of these traditions converges on the same truth: the crown is not only the highest center of perception but the meeting point between the human and the divine.

The spiraling petals themselves carry deep symbolic meaning. Unlike static symbols, the lotus is alive, constantly in motion, reflecting the dynamic nature of consciousness. The petals spiral as if following a cosmic dance, revealing that awakening is not a final event but an ongoing expansion into greater and greater wholeness. These spirals are mirrored in galaxies, in seashells, in the flow of energy itself. They remind us that the crown does not separate us from the world but connects us to its underlying patterns and rhythms. To experience the thousand-petaled flower is to recognize oneself as woven into the same tapestry of creation that spins the stars.

The rainbow light radiating from the lotus adds another dimension of meaning. White light, when refracted, reveals a spectrum of colors. In the same way, divine consciousness when expressed through the crown blossoms into countless forms and experiences. The rainbow symbolizes inclusivity, the union of all paths, all traditions, and all beings in one vast field of light. Each color carries its own healing resonance, weaving together into harmony. The seeker who sits beneath this radiant lotus becomes both a receiver and a transmitter of this rainbow frequency, radiating peace, compassion, and wisdom into the world.

Practically, connecting with the thousand-petaled lotus requires no elaborate ritual. It begins with stillness, a willingness to turn attention upward and inward. Breathing gently, one can visualize a luminous lotus above the head, glowing softly. With each breath, the petals open, releasing light. This is not imagination but a doorway into real experience. Over time, the visualization dissolves into felt presence. The crown begins to hum with subtle vibrations, and one perceives that wisdom is no longer something to be grasped but something that flows naturally through the open channel. In this state, the seeker becomes a vessel, and the thousand petals turn into pathways for light to descend and radiate outward.

The thousand-petaled lotus also teaches humility. To wear a crown of illumination is not to claim superiority but to embody service. Just as the flower blooms not for itself but for the world, the awakened crown opens not to elevate the ego but to allow the infinite to shine through. Those who have experienced the blossoming of the lotus often describe a deep sense of peace, compassion, and non-separation. The crown teaches that true illumination is not an escape from life but an embrace of it at its highest frequency.

The thousand-petaled flower is a mirror of your own infinite nature. Its unfolding is the unfolding of your being. Every petal that opens is a remembrance, every spiral a return to wholeness. To rest beneath its radiance is to know that you have never been apart from the source, that the light above you is the same light within you. The lotus is both a symbol and a lived reality, waiting for the moment when you are ready to open fully into the brilliance of the crown.

4.3.3 Crowns Across Traditions

Across the wide sweep of human history, cultures have envisioned light around the head as the ultimate sign of transcendence. The image of the crown is not limited to monarchs or rulers but is deeply tied to the recognition of divine radiance within a person. When the highest center of consciousness awakens, traditions describe it as fire, light, or blossoms bursting forth, and over the centuries artists, mystics, and storytellers have given this experience shape in luminous crowns.

In early Christianity, the halo became a visual code for sanctity. Saints were painted with golden circles encircling their heads, a sign that their consciousness had opened to divine illumination. The unbroken circle represented perfection and eternity, while the golden hue conveyed both spiritual wealth and the warmth of the divine sun. These depictions were not mere decoration but teachings in themselves, silently communicating that holiness shines outward as visible radiance.

In Buddhist traditions, the crown takes another form, often expressed as a flame rising from the head or a lotus blossoming above it. The Buddha is described as having a cranial protuberance known as the ushnisha, a symbolic crown that marks awakened wisdom. Iconography across Asia elaborated on this, surrounding enlightened beings with aureoles of rainbow-colored flames. These images remind practitioners that enlightenment is not only an inward realization but a light that transforms the space around them.

In Hinduism, the imagery of the sahasrara chakra, the thousand-petaled lotus, functions as both crown and gateway. Yogic texts describe this lotus as expanding endlessly, its petals shimmering with all colors of the spectrum. Deities and enlightened beings are shown with radiant headpieces or jewels glowing at the crown, representing access to cosmic consciousness. The crown here is not ornamental but functional, a conduit through which divine energy flows into the human vessel.

The ancient Egyptians held their own interpretation through crowns that combined earthly power with celestial meaning. The white and red crowns of Upper and Lower Egypt, when joined, symbolized unification, while solar disks placed atop divine figures marked their connection to the sun god Ra. These were not only signs of political authority but metaphysical emblems suggesting that the ruler was crowned with the fire of heaven itself.

In Persian and Zoroastrian traditions, the farr or divine glory was seen as a luminous halo around rulers and prophets. This glow was the visible proof that divine favor rested upon them. Similarly, in Jewish mysticism, stories of Moses describe his face shining so brightly after encountering the divine that he had to veil himself before the people. The crown of illumination in these narratives is not an external symbol but an overwhelming radiance too powerful to look upon directly.

In more mystical strands of Christianity, such as Eastern Orthodox hesychasm, the experience of the uncreated light was often described as a fiery crown or diadem that overwhelmed the senses. Saints who reported such encounters spoke of being clothed in light and crowned with brilliance. The iconographic tradition later showed this as halos made of concentric rings of gold and blue, echoing the vision of infinite light radiating from the divine source.

Even in indigenous and shamanic traditions, the head is marked as the portal of the sky. Headdresses of feathers, rays, or sunbursts often served not only as tribal insignia but as spiritual technology, imitating the natural crown of light perceived in altered states. The shaman's crown was a living symbol of connection to the upper worlds, affirming that the practitioner could channel wisdom from the heavens into the community.

What emerges across these traditions is a universality that transcends borders. Whether it is the halo of Christian saints, the lotus of Hindu yogis, the flame of Buddhist icons, or the feathered headdress of indigenous shamans, the imagery is consistent. The awakened human being is recognized by a radiance that emanates from the crown. This consistency suggests not mere cultural borrowing but a shared human perception, an archetypal recognition of how higher states of consciousness reveal themselves in light.

The crown archetype also serves as a reminder of responsibility. To be crowned is not only to bask in radiance but to serve as a bridge between heaven and earth. The luminous diadem, wherever it appears, symbolizes the integration of spiritual vision with earthly presence. It is a sign that illumination is not an escape from the world but an anointing that enables deeper service within it.

In contemplating these crowns across traditions, we begin to see that the image of light above the head is not simply religious decoration. It is a language of universality, a timeless way of expressing that the human vessel is designed to be crowned with radiance. To open the crown is to join a lineage of saints, mystics, prophets, and shamans who, in every corner of the world, have discovered that when consciousness flowers, it wears a crown of fire.

4.4 Comparative Keys of the Inner Kingdom

4.4.1 The Seven Lamps, Palaces, and Heavens

Throughout the sacred traditions of the world, there is a shared conviction that the human being is not merely flesh and bone but a temple of ascent, layered in stages of light. These stages have been described with different symbols: lamps in the Christian and Biblical imagination, palaces in Kabbalistic mysticism, and heavens in Islamic cosmology. Though the languages differ, each points to an inner cartography, a way of speaking about the journey of consciousness from earth to the heights of union.

In the Bible, the imagery of lamps appears repeatedly as signs of guidance and illumination. In the Book of Revelation, John speaks of the seven golden lampstands, which are often read as representing the seven churches, yet mystics have long suggested a more interior meaning. The lamp is a vessel that holds oil, and when lit it radiates light. Within the human frame, the lamp can be seen as the inner center that, once anointed, burns brightly with divine presence. Seven lamps suggest a complete system of illumination, a vertical sequence of centers within the temple of the body. Each lamp reveals another stage of clarity, leading the soul toward fullness of vision.

The Kabbalistic tradition carries a parallel teaching through the concept of the seven palaces, known in Hebrew as *Heichalot*. These palaces are described in ancient mystical writings as levels or chambers through which the soul ascends in meditation and prayer. Each palace contains trials, guardians, and secrets that must be navigated by the seeker. The journey through the palaces is not geographical but spiritual, demanding purity of heart, integrity of intention, and courage of spirit. Like the lamps, the palaces mark stages of progression, yet their imagery emphasizes not only light but the architecture of the inner temple. To move from one palace to another is to pass through a threshold, gaining access to deeper mysteries of the divine.

Islamic mysticism, particularly within the Sufi tradition, speaks of seven heavens. The Qur'an itself refers to the creation of seven heavens layered above one another, and in mystical interpretation these become levels of spiritual consciousness. Each heaven corresponds to a higher refinement of the soul, a greater nearness to the Divine. In ascension narratives, such as the Prophet Muhammad's Night Journey (*Isra and Mi'raj*), the heavens are revealed as luminous realms where prophets dwell, each heaven signifying another step on the ladder of union with God. The heavens are radiant, expansive, and filled with angelic presence, echoing the image of lamps and palaces as spheres of light.

When the three traditions are placed side by side, their unity becomes clear. The seven lamps symbolize centers of inner light, the palaces mark thresholds of spiritual transformation, and the heavens describe the vast expansion of consciousness as it rises toward the divine throne. All three use the language of sevens, a sacred number that speaks of completion and fullness. Sevens appear in days of creation, in Sabbaths, in cycles of prophecy and revelation. To structure the path of ascent in seven stages is to say that the journey is both total and divinely patterned.

The commonality does not end with number. All three traditions place emphasis on preparation and purity. A lamp must be filled with oil before it can burn. A palace requires a worthy traveler to be admitted. A heaven is opened only to those who have refined their hearts. The symbolism insists that ascent is not achieved by force or intellect alone, but by alignment of the soul with the qualities of light: love, mercy, humility, and surrender.

These stages also highlight the interplay between human participation and divine grace. The seeker must tend the lamp, walk the palace halls, and yearn for the heavens, yet the illumination that allows each step to open is a gift from above. This balance is central to mystical teaching: human effort prepares the vessel, but divine fire ignites it. Without oil, the lamp cannot burn, but without the spark, the oil remains dormant.

Comparative Map of the Sevenfold Ascent

Tradition	Symbol	Stage/Level	Description	Spiritual Quality
Biblical	Seven Lamps	Lamps filled with oil	Centers of light within the inner temple, each requiring anointing to shine	Illumination, guidance, faithfulness
Kabbalistic	Seven Palaces (*Heichalot*)	Palatial chambers of ascent	Mystical halls guarded by thresholds, each unveiling deeper divine mysteries	Purity, integrity, courage
Islamic/Sufi	Seven Heavens	Expansive luminous realms	Layers of spiritual consciousness, encountered in ascension narratives	Nearness to God, refinement of soul, surrender

Mystics across traditions have also warned that these stages are not abstract doctrines but living realities within. A lamp may correspond to the heart opening, a palace to the clearing of a psychological barrier, a heaven to the expansion of perception in prayer. The seven stages therefore become a map of transformation that is lived and embodied, not merely studied. To contemplate them is to align one's own journey with the wisdom of centuries, to recognize that the inner kingdom is structured, layered, and meant to be ascended step by step.

When we compare the lamps, palaces, and heavens, we glimpse a universal key: human beings everywhere have intuited that the soul is called to rise, and that rise is marked by sacred thresholds. The language changes with culture and scripture, yet the inner vision is the same. The journey begins in the dimness of the earthly temple and ends in the radiance of divine presence, crowned with light.

4.4.2 Archetypal Keys and Portals

Across the world's traditions and mythologies, the image of a key, a door, or a gate recurs as a profound archetype. These are not mere objects of physical passage, but thresholds between states of being. A key suggests hiddenness, something that is not immediately accessible but requires the right alignment to open. A door symbolizes the liminal space where one reality ends and another begins. A gate often carries guardianship, reminding the seeker that transformation demands readiness. Together, they express the universal principle of initiation: to step into a greater dimension, one must first find, and then turn, the key.

In the ancient Near East, kings were described as holders of keys, not just to treasure houses but to wisdom itself. To be entrusted with a key was to be seen as trustworthy enough to enter a chamber of mystery. In Egyptian symbolism, the ankh served as a living key, a shape combining circle and cross that opened the way to eternal life. In Christianity, the handing of keys to Peter represents spiritual authority, not to dominate, but to bind and to loose, to open the way of reconciliation and to close the way of ignorance. In Islam, the very name of the first chapter of the Qur'an, *Al-Fatiha*, is translated as "The Opening," positioning revelation itself as a key that unlocks divine nearness.

Doors also carry layered meanings across traditions. In the Vedic texts, the human body is often called a house of nine doors, representing the physical orifices, but only through the hidden tenth door does liberation occur. This tenth gate, sometimes depicted as at the crown of the head, reveals that not all doors are the same: some are pathways to the outer world, while one leads inward to the infinite. In medieval mysticism, doorways were linked to humility and prayer, for one could not pass through the narrow gate unless willing to bow. This recognition turns the door into a test: can the ego diminish itself enough to enter?

Gates are perhaps the most dramatic of all. They are never neutral spaces but guarded thresholds. In Mesopotamian myth, Inanna must pass through seven gates to descend into the underworld, each requiring her to surrender a piece of her power until she is laid bare. In Kabbalistic writings, the Gates of Light are stages of revelation, each more radiant but also more demanding. In Chinese tradition, the "Heavenly Gate" in the body corresponds to the governing vessel, the channel that opens one to cosmic energy. Gates are thus simultaneously protective and transformative: they keep the unprepared out and prepare the ready by the act of crossing.

Keys, doors, and gates converge in the human interior. The key is intention, faith, and resonance. The door is the place in consciousness where an old self must end for a new self to begin. The gate is the actual crossing into a more expanded reality, often accompanied by resistance, fear, or awe. Many initiation rites across cultures enact these symbols: the initiate is blindfolded (facing the closed door), given words of power or objects (receiving the key), and finally led across a threshold into a new circle (passing through the gate). The outer act mirrors the inner transformation, showing that these images live not only in myth but in psychology and practice.

Modern seekers can still recognize these archetypes in their own journeys. A decision to release an old habit may feel like standing before a door. Finding the inner courage to continue may be like discovering a hidden key. And the moment of irreversible choice, when one steps forward despite uncertainty, is the gate itself. Once passed, life never feels quite the same. The seeker senses that something has been left behind, and something greater has been entered.

These symbols also explain why wisdom traditions guard certain teachings. Not everything is meant to be accessed without preparation, just as not every door in a sacred temple is meant to be opened casually. The presence of keys and gates protects what is holy by ensuring that those who enter have attuned themselves. But once entered, the mystery does not merely grant knowledge; it reshapes the one who has crossed. To be given the key is to be trusted with transformation.

Archetypal keys and portals remind us that spiritual growth is not passive. It requires searching, readiness, and willingness to cross. The keys are often already within us, hidden as qualities of love, courage, and surrender. The doors appear at the edges of our comfort, and the gates stand before the mysteries we long for yet fear. To walk this path is to recognize that every threshold is sacred. Each key discovered, each door opened, and each gate crossed is another step toward the inner kingdom that has awaited us all along.

4.5 A Practical Contemplation

4.5.1 Visualization of the Seven Seals

Close your eyes and settle into stillness. Take three deep breaths, inhaling slowly through the nose, and exhaling with ease. With each breath, imagine the body as a standing temple, a vertical column of light. Within this temple are seven radiant seals, luminous centers aligned from base to crown. This practice is a way of awakening each seal by touching it with awareness, color, and vibration.

Begin at the base of the spine. Visualize a glowing red sphere pulsing like a living ember. Sense its stability and grounding, as though roots extend deep into the earth. On the inhale, draw strength from the earth itself. On the exhale, whisper the sound "LAM" softly or silently, feeling the seal begin to hum with vitality.

Move upward to the second seal, just below the navel. Envision a bright orange sphere glowing like a sunrise over water. It swirls gently, reminding you of flow, creativity, and the pleasure of being alive. Inhale as if drawing a wave of orange light into the body. Exhale the sound "VAM" and feel the seal shimmer like liquid fire.

Now shift awareness to the third seal, located at the solar plexus. A golden sphere appears, radiant like the sun at midday. This is the seat of will and inner power. Inhale golden light that strengthens the core of your being. Exhale the sound "RAM" and feel the flame of confidence and clarity rising within.

Continue to the fourth seal at the center of the chest. A glowing green sphere blooms like an emerald flower. Inhale deeply, filling the heart with tenderness and compassion. Exhale the sound "YAM" and allow the green light to spread outward, embracing yourself and all beings. The fifth seal resides at the throat. See a luminous blue sphere spinning like a clear sky. Inhale coolness and openness. Exhale the sound "HAM" and feel the throat open as a channel of truth and expression, a sacred instrument for authentic voice.

At the forehead rests the sixth seal, indigo and deep as twilight. Inhale into the center of the brow, sensing the presence of inner vision. Exhale the sound "OM," allowing the indigo light to sharpen awareness and open the inner eye. Finally, turn to the crown of the head. Above you, a violet or white sphere opens like a luminous halo. Inhale radiant light from above, feeling it pour into your being. Exhale silently and simply rest in stillness, letting the light dissolve into boundless presence.

When all seven seals are lit, imagine them aligned like jewels on a staff of light. Breathe gently, letting the column glow as a single stream. For a moment, rest in the unity of the whole. The body is now the temple, the seals its living lamps. When you are ready, return slowly. Bring awareness to the breath, the body, and the room around you. Carry the memory of these colors and sounds with you, knowing they remain alive within, ready to be rekindled at any moment.

4.5.2 Breathing the Language of Light

Sit comfortably with the spine upright, either on a cushion or a chair, and close your eyes. Place one hand gently over your heart and the other over your lower abdomen. Take three long, slow breaths, allowing your awareness to sink inward. This practice is about more than oxygen, it is about receiving light through breath, allowing luminous currents of script and pattern to enter and harmonize your whole being.

As you inhale, imagine that the air around you is not empty but alive with radiant letters of light. These are not ordinary letters but streams of glowing script, flowing symbols that resemble fire and wind woven

together. They drift toward you as if carried on invisible currents. With each breath in, see them entering through the nostrils as golden and silver filaments, descending into the lungs like living poetry.

Feel these letters dissolve into shimmering light within the chest. They do not remain static; they rearrange and dance, forming luminous patterns that spiral into the heart center. Rest your awareness on this inner image: the heart glowing with letters that breathe and move, a silent song written not in ink but in radiance.

On the exhale, imagine the light expanding outward. Instead of leaving you, it fills your body. See streams of luminous script traveling upward to the head, softening the mind, and downward into the belly, grounding your inner fire. With each outward breath, the letters dissolve into pure brightness that permeates your whole being, harmonizing thought, feeling, and breath as one.

After a few cycles, deepen the visualization. With each inhale, see letters entering as glowing rivers of light, sometimes appearing as Hebrew, Sanskrit, Arabic, or other sacred alphabets, yet beyond any single language. They are universal codes, shapes born of light itself. As you receive them, do not try to "read" them with the eyes of the mind. Instead, feel

35

them with the soul. Notice how some letters bring calm, others awaken warmth, others expand clarity. Now imagine that the inhaled letters gather into a sphere of light within the heart. It pulses with every breath, expanding and contracting gently. As it glows brighter, the letters dissolve into pure radiance until there is no separation between symbol and light. You are not "reading" the script, you are becoming it, embodying the language of light with every inhale and exhale. For the final stage, allow the breath to slow naturally.

Each inhale invites luminous currents inward, each exhale allows them to merge with your essence. Rest in the sensation that you are both the reader and the book, both the breath and the light. The practice is complete when you sense a deep quietude, a subtle knowing that something within has been harmonized without effort. Carry this awareness with you. Even when your eyes are open and the day is busy, remember that each breath can be luminous, each word spoken can echo the hidden script of light flowing through you.

Chapter 5 – The Path of Embodiment

5.1 From Knowing to Becoming

Knowledge has always been revered. Humanity builds libraries, archives, and now digital clouds that contain vast reservoirs of information. Yet knowledge, in itself, is not transformation. To collect truths without embodying them is like gathering seeds but never planting them in the soil. The journey of the inner temple is not about what you know but about what you become. Knowing is the threshold, but becoming is the path that changes your reality.

When you first encounter higher truths, they often arrive as ideas. You hear a phrase, you read a scripture, or you sense a whisper that resonates. This is the spark of recognition, a reminder of something already within you. But unless that spark is nurtured, it remains only a thought. True growth requires allowing knowledge to sink below the mind into the deeper currents of your being.

Becoming demands integration. It is when the words no longer float on the surface but echo through your choices, your gestures, your way of breathing. To know that light dwells in you is one thing; to walk as one who carries light is another. The first requires belief, the second requires embodiment. It is embodiment that turns knowledge into living wisdom.

The ancients often taught in symbols because symbols bypass the mind's hunger for endless analysis and go directly to the heart. A flame does not explain itself. It shines. To embody knowledge is to stop holding truth at a distance, as an object to study, and instead allow it to infuse you. This is why disciplines like prayer, meditation, fasting, and ritual were preserved across cultures. They take truths out of the realm of theory and make them tangible in the rhythm of daily life.

Many seekers remain caught in the cycle of collecting. They read, they attend workshops, they absorb concepts, but their lives show little change. This is the difference between sitting beside a river and actually drinking the water. The river may be beautiful, its sound soothing, but only when you drink does it become part of you. The path of becoming is not about how much you know but about how deeply you have allowed what you know to transform your being.

One of the greatest challenges is the ego's subtle attachment to information. The ego loves to claim knowledge as a possession. It wants to say, "I understand this system, I have studied that tradition, I can quote this teaching." Yet truth resists being owned. The moment you attempt to hold it, it slips beyond your grasp. Truth is not content for the mind to display but a living current to be surrendered to. Embodiment requires humility, the willingness to let truth work on you rather than you trying to control it.

This is why becoming often feels less like acquiring and more like unlearning. You let go of false layers, rigid definitions, and the need to prove. You soften into presence. In that presence, knowledge dissolves into direct experience. You no longer repeat the phrase "I am light," you feel luminous. You no longer debate about the divine breath, you breathe with reverence. You no longer theorize about compassion, you embody it in your gaze, your tone, your actions.

Embodiment is also a path of consistency. Just as a seed requires daily sunlight and water, truths require daily tending. The flame of awareness is not sustained by intensity alone but by steady devotion. Many begin the path with great enthusiasm but falter because they seek sudden transformation without ongoing practice. Becoming is gradual. It is the shaping of your inner temple brick by brick, day by day. Small daily choices, repeated with sincerity, form the architecture of a new reality.

There is also a paradox in embodiment. The more you become, the less you feel the need to declare what you have become. The sage does not boast of wisdom, the healer does not announce healing at every turn. Embodiment speaks through presence. Others sense it, not because of your words, but because of the energy you emanate. To walk into a room with quiet integrity is more powerful than to announce your beliefs. Presence becomes the testimony.

From knowing to becoming is the essential crossing. Knowledge alone can become stagnant. Becoming keeps it alive, fluid, breathing. You are not here to memorize truths but to radiate them. Not to catalog symbols but to live as one. When knowledge becomes flesh, when truth flows in your pulse, when wisdom shines through your eyes, you have stepped onto the true path of the inner kingdom.

5.2 Rituals for the Daily Temple

If the body is a temple, then each day is a liturgy. The way you rise, breathe, eat, walk, and rest are not merely habits, they are offerings laid upon the inner altar. To embody higher truth is to consecrate the ordinary. Rituals are the bridge between the sacred and the daily, ensuring that illumination does not remain confined to fleeting moments of meditation but permeates every hour of your life.

The ancients understood that the human being is not transformed by sporadic bursts of devotion but by steady rhythm. Sunrises and sunsets mark the heavens with a pulse, tides move in cycles, seasons unfold in spirals. The soul too is shaped by rhythm. When you create daily rituals aligned with your intention, you synchronize your inner life with the cosmic pattern. This does not mean constructing elaborate ceremonies. The most transformative rituals are often the simplest, repeated with reverence.

One of the foundational rituals is the act of awakening. To open your eyes in the morning is to be given life anew. Many rise hurriedly, already consumed by tasks and noise. But what if the very first breath of the day was an act of remembrance? A conscious inhalation of gratitude, a whispered affirmation, or even a silent pause facing the light of the dawn. In that moment, the mundane becomes sacred. You no longer simply wake up, you enter the temple.

Cleansing rituals also carry profound significance. Across cultures, water has been seen as a purifier and renewer. Bathing, washing the face, or even drinking a glass of clear water can be more than hygiene. When performed with intention, it becomes symbolic of releasing the old and preparing for the new. Each drop becomes a reminder that you are not static but in constant renewal.

Movement is another form of ritual. Whether it is yoga, walking, stretching, or bowing, the body in motion can embody prayer. Movements that are slow, intentional, and aligned with the breath remind the body that it is not merely a vessel but a living sanctuary. Even simple gestures, like placing a hand on the heart before speaking or bowing the head before eating, reframe action as sacred participation.

The ritual of nourishment is equally central. Food is the daily communion with the earth's abundance. To eat unconsciously is to reduce it to fuel. To eat with awareness is to recognize it as a gift. Saying a blessing, even in silence, transforms a meal into a sacrament. Chewing slowly, tasting fully, and receiving with gratitude allows the act of eating to echo the greater truth that all life is interconnected.

Silence itself can be cultivated as a ritual. In a world saturated with noise, the deliberate choice to hold moments of stillness is deeply countercultural. A pause before speaking, a minute of quiet before entering a meeting, a few breaths of silence before sleep, these are the ways the temple protects its sanctity. Silence is not absence, it is presence in its purest form. The setting sun offers another opportunity. Just as mornings invite intention, evenings invite reflection. To look back upon the day with honesty, to release what must be released, and to carry forward what must be remembered, is to close the temple doors with reverence. Whether through journaling, prayer, or simple contemplation, the evening ritual ensures that the day does not pass unnoticed but becomes a thread woven consciously into the greater tapestry of your life.

Rituals also guard the flame. The inner fire of awareness flickers when neglected. But when tended, it glows steadily, illuminating both your inner chambers and the world around you. The guardianship of that flame depends less on dramatic spiritual acts and more on consistent daily devotion. The daily temple is not about rigid discipline, but about living in a way that constantly renews your covenant with the sacred within.

Importantly, rituals are not chains but pathways. They are not meant to confine you but to liberate your attention. When practiced with authenticity, they bring fluidity rather than rigidity. A ritual loses its essence when it becomes mechanical. The power lies not in the act itself but in the awareness infused into it. Lighting a candle without presence is just a gesture; lighting it with the intention to invite clarity transforms the flame into a beacon. Creating personal rituals is an art. While traditions offer guidance, the most meaningful rituals are those that resonate with your own spirit. For some, it may be chanting a sacred word at sunrise. For others, it may be writing down a single line of gratitude before sleep. What matters is not complexity but sincerity. A ritual must speak to your soul, not simply mimic someone else's.

The cumulative effect of daily rituals is profound. Over time, they reshape not only your habits but your identity. You cease to see yourself as someone occasionally visiting the temple of the sacred. You begin to recognize yourself as the temple itself. Every act, from breath to speech to step, becomes a continuation of the inner liturgy. And as you live in this rhythm, others will sense it — not through your declarations, but through the quiet radiance of your presence.

The path of embodiment requires anchoring truth in the ordinary. Rituals are the anchors. They ground you in the eternal while you walk in the temporal. They weave light into the fabric of time. They remind you that spirituality is not apart from life but at the heart of it. Each day, with its rising and setting sun, becomes not a cycle to endure but a ceremony to live.

5.3 Guardianship of the Flame

Within the depths of every human being there exists a flame that does not belong to the external world. It is neither born of wood nor sustained by oil, yet it burns with a radiance that refuses extinction. This inner flame is a symbol of consciousness itself, the spark of awareness that links us to the source of life. Across traditions, the image of fire has been used to describe purity, vigilance, and the power to illuminate darkness. Guardianship of the flame, then, is not only a metaphor for spiritual responsibility but also a lived practice of honoring and protecting what is most essential within.

The flame represents the soul's vitality and integrity. It is that part of you that refuses to be defined by fear, cynicism, or despair. When you allow it to burn steadily, it becomes the guiding light through confusion, the warmth in seasons of coldness, and the energy that fuels transformation. But unlike a fire in the material world, this flame can dim when neglected, hidden beneath the ashes of distraction or smothered by the winds of negativity. Guardianship calls for awareness and discipline, not as burdens but as forms of devotion.

Ancient initiatory schools often placed fire at the center of their rites. In the temples of Egypt, the priests tended eternal lamps as a sign of cosmic order. In Zoroastrian practice, sacred fire embodied truth and was watched with great reverence. In Christian mysticism, the flame became the presence of divine love descending at Pentecost. To guard the flame was to safeguard the transmission of wisdom itself, for as long as the fire burned, the covenant between heaven and earth remained unbroken. When you picture the flame in your own life, you step into this lineage of responsibility.

Guardianship is first about recognition. Many pass through life unaware that such a fire even exists within them. They look outward for meaning and stability, overlooking the simple truth that everything they seek is already burning softly in their chest. To recognize the flame is to pause in silence, to close the eyes, and to feel the warmth of being itself. It is subtle, but once known, it cannot be forgotten. You realize that no matter how deep the darkness around you, there is something untouchable at your core.

Yet recognition is not enough. A guardian must learn the arts of tending. The flame thrives on clarity, focus, and inner alignment. Practices such as meditation, breath awareness, or sacred recitation serve as fuel, steadying the flame against the pull of restlessness. Negative habits, by contrast, scatter its light. Excessive indulgence, dishonesty, or chronic distraction act like gusts of wind, destabilizing what should remain constant. Guardianship is therefore both protective and creative. You defend against what harms the flame and also feed it with what allows it to grow brighter.

Another aspect of guardianship is humility. To hold a flame in cupped hands is to admit its fragility. You do not grasp it tightly, for that would extinguish it. You do not ignore it, for that would let it die. Instead, you hover in the balance between reverence and trust, acknowledging that the flame is not yours to own but yours to steward. This humility softens the ego and awakens gratitude, reminding you that the most profound treasures are not possessions but gifts entrusted to your care.

Guardianship also extends beyond the self. The flame within you is linked to the flame within others. To guard your own light is to contribute to a larger network of fire that sustains humanity's collective journey. Acts of kindness, truth, and courage do not remain isolated; they ignite other flames. In this way, guardianship transforms into service. You carry your light not as a personal ornament but as a beacon for those still searching in the dark.

There are moments when the flame feels small, flickering against overwhelming challenges. Yet even the smallest light can redefine an entire landscape of shadows. Guardianship does not demand perfection, only constancy. Each time you choose integrity over compromise, presence over distraction, love over bitterness, you strengthen the flame. Over years, this devotion shapes a life of inner radiance. Others may not see the hours of quiet tending, but they feel the warmth when they stand near you.

To live as a guardian of the flame is to remember that your deepest essence is both luminous and enduring. You carry within you a fire that is eternal, yet it relies on your daily attentiveness to remain vibrant. This is the paradox and the invitation: the flame is indestructible in its essence yet entrusted to your hands in its expression. You are both the keeper and the kept, the one who guards and the one transformed by guarding.

The practice of guardianship is simple but profound. Begin each day by envisioning the flame between your palms, golden and steady. Whisper to it your intention to protect what is sacred, to use your energy wisely, to radiate warmth to others. Throughout the day, notice when the flame dims and what restores it. By night, offer gratitude for its presence, even if faint. Over time, you will find that the flame teaches you more than any words can: that life's true power lies not in conquest or accumulation but in carrying light faithfully through the shifting landscapes of existence.

5.4 A Practice of Embodiment

Embodiment is not an abstract idea but a lived process of anchoring light, presence, and awareness in the body. Too often spiritual work remains in the mind, circling in concepts and visions, while the body waits for its share of the awakening. This practice is a gentle invitation to unify knowing with being, thought with breath, and intention with flesh. It requires no elaborate tools or settings, only a willingness to be fully here.

Begin by choosing a quiet space where you feel safe and undisturbed. Sit comfortably with your back straight, feet touching the ground, and hands resting on your lap. Close your eyes and bring your attention to the rhythm of your breathing. Inhale deeply through the nose, filling the belly first, then the chest, and exhale slowly through the mouth. Allow the breath to carry away distractions and settle you into the present moment. Continue this for several cycles until your body feels relaxed and your mind grows still.

Now, gently shift your awareness to the crown of your head. Imagine a soft stream of luminous energy flowing downward like warm sunlight. Let it wash over your head, shoulders, chest, and down through your torso, legs, and feet. With each breath, picture this light weaving into your cells, infusing your body with harmony. As you breathe in, silently affirm, "I receive." As you exhale, affirm, "I embody." This rhythm becomes a mantra, a cycle of receiving and anchoring.

Next, focus on your heart. Place one hand over it and notice its beat. Envision a golden flame within, small but steady. With each breath, allow this flame to grow brighter, filling your chest with warmth. Recognize this flame as the signal of your essence, the unbroken spark that bridges spirit and matter. Whisper to yourself, "I carry the flame." Stay with this image until you sense your whole body resonating with its glow.

Now expand your awareness outward. Feel the weight of your body pressing into the ground, the air brushing against your skin, the subtle hum of life surrounding you. Imagine that the same golden flame within your heart is mirrored in every cell, in the earth beneath you, and in the sky above. Sense the unity between inner and outer, between what you feel and what is.

To conclude, slowly open your eyes. Place both hands gently over your heart and bow your head slightly in gratitude. Take three final breaths, each one deeper than the last, affirming silently, "I embody presence. I embody truth. I embody light."

Practicing embodiment daily, even for a few minutes, turns knowledge into lived reality. It steadies the spirit, strengthens the body, and teaches the mind that wisdom is not only to be understood but to be lived. Over time, this practice roots illumination in every step, gesture, and word, making life itself the temple where spirit abides.

Closing Reflection – The First Door Opens

Every journey through the inner kingdom begins with a threshold. To cross it requires more than curiosity; it requires readiness. What you have walked through in these chapters is not simply a set of concepts or symbols but a series of keys that invite you to open the first true door within. This door does not appear in stone or wood, nor does it swing on hinges. It opens inward, in the heart, and once you step through, the landscape of your existence begins to shift in ways that cannot be reversed.

When the ancients spoke of initiation, they spoke of thresholds such as this. In the myths of every culture, the seeker comes to a gateway guarded by riddles, serpents, flames, or lions. What is being guarded is not a place but a level of consciousness. The guardian is not external but a reflection of your own resistance, your doubts, your fears of becoming more than you currently are. To open the first door, then, is to look directly into those doubts and choose trust. It is the moment when the soul whispers, "I am ready to be more."

This door is called "the first" not because it is small or unimportant but because it is the one upon which all others depend. To open it is to choose embodiment over theory, practice over abstraction, love over hesitation. Without this opening, teachings remain words on a page. With it, words transform into living fire. You begin to feel a resonance in your body, a shift in your perception, a new lightness in how you meet the world. What once seemed symbolic starts to feel undeniably real.

Pause and recall what has stirred you most deeply in this exploration. Was it the image of the seven seals glowing along the body? Was it the luminous language flowing like script across the inner sky? Was it the flame cupped within the hands of guardianship? Whatever touched you most is not just a metaphor. It is your personal door, a point of entry designed for your soul. To honor it is to listen and respond. To ignore it is to postpone what is already calling your name.

Crossing the first door is rarely dramatic in the outer world. You may not see visions, nor hear a voice announcing the passage. Instead, you may notice subtle yet unmistakable changes: an ease in your breathing when you release old worries, a quiet confidence when you speak truth, a sensation of alignment when your actions match your deeper knowing. These are the footsteps across the threshold. They are signs that something within you has shifted from seeking to being.

It is important to understand that the first door is not about perfection. Many fear they cannot walk through because they are not pure enough, wise enough, or strong enough. Yet the threshold itself is the teacher. You do not need to be complete before you begin; you begin in order to be transformed. The door opens not for the flawless but for the willing. Every step beyond it will refine, strengthen, and illuminate you in ways you could not have achieved by waiting.

Once inside, a new dimension of life begins to unfold. You will still encounter challenges, but they appear differently now. Obstacles no longer seem like punishments but like mirrors, showing you the parts of yourself that long to be integrated. Relationships become arenas of growth rather than battles for validation. The body becomes an ally instead of a burden. Even silence shifts, becoming a space where presence speaks louder than thought.

This is why traditions speak of the "first door" as sacred. It changes the map entirely. Before, life may have felt like a collection of unrelated events. After, life feels like a woven tapestry where every thread carries meaning. The same daily rituals—breathing, eating, speaking, resting—become opportunities to embody spirit. Nothing is wasted; everything belongs. You no longer walk as someone seeking to arrive but as someone who is already home, discovering deeper rooms within the house of the self.

The first door also awakens responsibility. With greater awareness comes the invitation to live differently. You may feel called to release habits that dull your clarity, to speak truth where silence once held you back, or to nurture the flame of compassion when judgment rises. This is the guardianship of the flame: carrying the light of your own awakening and protecting it against the winds of distraction or fear. Responsibility here does not mean burden but devotion. It is the joy of tending what is precious.

To sustain this opening, practice is essential. Small, consistent acts anchor the new awareness: breathing consciously in moments of stress, pausing to sense the flame in your heart, allowing silence to be a teacher, blessing the body with care and gratitude. These are not lofty or complex actions, but they are profound when lived daily. Over time, they keep the door open, ensuring you do not retreat into the old house of forgetfulness.

And so we return to you, standing at your own threshold. The door has appeared because you sought it, or perhaps because it sought you. The question is not whether you are ready but whether you are willing. Willingness is the true key, the vibration that dissolves the lock. You may feel hesitation, but within that hesitation is the very energy you need to step forward.

As you stand here, breathe deeply. Imagine the golden flame rising from your heart, illuminating the path before you. Feel the presence of those who have walked this way before, countless seekers across centuries who also faced their first threshold. You are not alone; the path is well-trodden, and the light you carry joins theirs in a lineage of awakening.

When you step through, do so with humility and with courage. Bow slightly to the guardians, whether they appear as fear, as doubt, or as silence. Thank them for reminding you that what lies ahead is precious. Then, with steady breath, lift your gaze and walk forward. The threshold dissolves behind you, and the world within expands infinitely before you.

This is the first door. It is both an ending and a beginning. An ending of living in separation, a beginning of living in unity. An ending of theory, a beginning of embodiment. An ending of seeking, a beginning of being.

The first door opens not just once but continually. Each day you rise and choose presence, you open it again. Each act of love reaffirms the passage. Each moment of stillness expands the threshold into a palace of light. You will discover that there are many doors ahead, but none will matter without the courage to step through this one.

And so the reflection becomes an invitation. Do not leave this door as an image on a page. Close your eyes, breathe, and feel it now. Place your hand on your heart and whisper the words that awaken passage: *I am willing.* In that moment, the door opens, and the journey truly begins.

Book of Wisdom – Volume II

Introduction – Beyond the Veil

Every seeker who arrives at this point has already walked through the first garden of wisdom. The foundations have been laid, the keys of the inner kingdom have been touched, and the language of symbols has begun to open its doors. Yet knowledge, no matter how profound, is never the destination. It is the lamp that illuminates the path beyond the visible horizon. Volume II of the *Book of Wisdom* invites you into that horizon. It is not simply a continuation, but an expansion into deeper waters, a journey beyond the veil of ordinary perception.

The veil is a mystery in itself. It is spoken of in the temples of Egypt, where the initiate approached the hidden chambers with eyes veiled and heart burning with longing. It appears in the scriptures of many traditions, as the curtain separating the sacred from the profane, the holy of holies from the common ground. It is also within us, as the thin layer of forgetting that allows us to live in the material world without constantly being overwhelmed by the immensity of the eternal. To move beyond the veil is not to abandon life, but to discover that life itself is more luminous, more layered, and more interconnected than it appears.

This second volume is an invitation to that unveiling. Here, we are no longer satisfied with outer explanations or surface-level interpretations. We will step into the advanced mysteries that demand not only intellectual attention but the participation of the whole being. They require courage, because the veil does not simply conceal knowledge; it protects the seeker until they are ready. The lifting of the veil is always a birth, and like all births, it comes with both pain and ecstasy, with endings and beginnings intertwined.

The journey you are about to enter is not linear. It moves in spirals, weaving together traditions, archetypes, and inner practices that echo one another across cultures and centuries. In these pages, you will encounter the mystery of time and its cycles, the deeper structures of sound and light, the archetypes of death and rebirth, the hidden maps of the subtle body, and the transmissions that have always existed beyond words. You will see how sages, mystics, and visionaries across the world described the same landscapes of the soul in different languages, each pointing to the ineffable.

Yet this book is not meant only to inform. It is designed as a mirror and a threshold. You will find passages that read like teachings, others that read like riddles, and still others that act like silent companions, bypassing the intellect to stir something in your spirit. This is because wisdom is not a collection of facts. It is a living current, and to approach it requires not just reading but allowing yourself to be read by the text. Every word, every image, every practice is a key. Whether the door opens depends not on the page but on your willingness to receive.

Beyond the veil, certainty dissolves. What you thought you knew about yourself, about reality, even about the divine, may be overturned. Here paradox reigns: the path is both narrow and infinite, the journey is both deeply personal and universally shared, the truths revealed are both timeless and unfolding in this very moment. To walk this path requires the ability to hold opposites without collapsing into confusion. It asks you to dwell in the fertile tension between what is known and what is still hidden. This is the alchemy of transformation.

Some may wonder, why advance into deeper mysteries at all? Is it not enough to live simply, to love, to act with kindness? Indeed, these are the highest teachings, and one can live a fulfilled life without ever seeking beyond. But for those who feel the pull of the hidden, who sense that the surface is only the beginning, the mysteries become not a luxury but a necessity. The soul hungers for depth, for remembrance, for contact with the eternal. Ignoring this hunger is possible, but it creates a restlessness that no outer success can soothe. Answering it brings peace, not because all questions are resolved, but because the questions themselves are transfigured into living companions.

As you move through this book, consider it a map, but a map unlike any other. It does not lead you from point A to point B. Instead, it reveals the landscapes already present within you. You will encounter images of the crown of illumination, the thousand-petaled lotus, the gates of fire, the rivers of memory. Each of these is both symbolic and real. They are patterns of consciousness, archetypal structures that shape the very way we experience existence. By contemplating them, you begin to awaken to dimensions of yourself that were always present but dormant.

There is a danger here, and it must be spoken of. To walk beyond the veil is to encounter not only light but also shadow. The deeper the light, the deeper the shadow that accompanies it. Traditions have always warned that seekers who rush forward without grounding risk being consumed by illusions, inflations, or despair. This is why the path must be walked with humility, with patience, and with the support of practices that root you in the body, in breath, in simple presence. Wisdom is not found by escaping the human but by embodying it fully. The veil lifts not when you reject life but when you embrace it as sacred.

And so, as we step into this journey together, hold close three guiding principles. The first is openness. Let go of rigid categories, of the need to fit every symbol into a tidy explanation. The second is discernment. Not every inner vision or idea is wisdom; some are projections of desire or fear. Learn to feel the difference, to test the fruit by its taste. The third is devotion. Without love, the mysteries remain closed. It is love that makes the veil porous, that allows the light beyond to shine through.

This introduction is itself a threshold. You stand before the veil, sensing its texture, its shimmer, its invitation. You know there is more, though you may not yet see it. That knowing is enough. Trust that what awaits is not foreign but deeply familiar. The veil conceals not to deny you, but to prepare you for the wonder that is about to unfold.

The journey beyond the veil is a journey into remembrance: remembering that you are more than a body, more than a story, more than a single lifetime. It is remembering that the flame within you is the same flame that has guided seekers across ages. It is remembering that every symbol is a doorway, every breath a prayer, every moment a chance to embody the eternal.

Now the threshold is before you. The curtain trembles. The first door opens once again, but this time it does not lead back to what you already know. It leads into the great mystery, the vast unknown, the luminous depth that calls you by name. Breathe, step forward, and allow the veil to part. The journey beyond has already begun.

Chapter 6 – The Cosmic Mirror

6.1 Above as Within

The ancients often spoke of the heavens not as distant stars scattered in a cold void, but as living reflections of the soul. The phrase "as above, so below" has echoed through hermetic texts, mystical traditions, and poetic visions, yet its deeper meaning is rarely grasped. To say that what lies above mirrors what lies within is to affirm that there is no separation between cosmos and consciousness. The same principles that order galaxies pulse in the rhythm of your breath. The same harmonies that bind

constellations into patterns are woven into the threads of your thoughts and emotions. The mirror does not exist out there; it is within the very fabric of your being. Look at the night sky. Its vastness seems overwhelming, a measureless expanse in which one might feel small. Yet when reflected upon still waters, the stars become intimate, shimmering in reach of your hand. This is the first secret of the cosmic mirror: the outer is only revealed when inner waters are still. In turbulence, reflection breaks into distortion. In calmness, the infinite sky settles into the depths of the heart. To cultivate inner stillness is not escapism but alignment, a preparation for seeing truth without fragmentation.

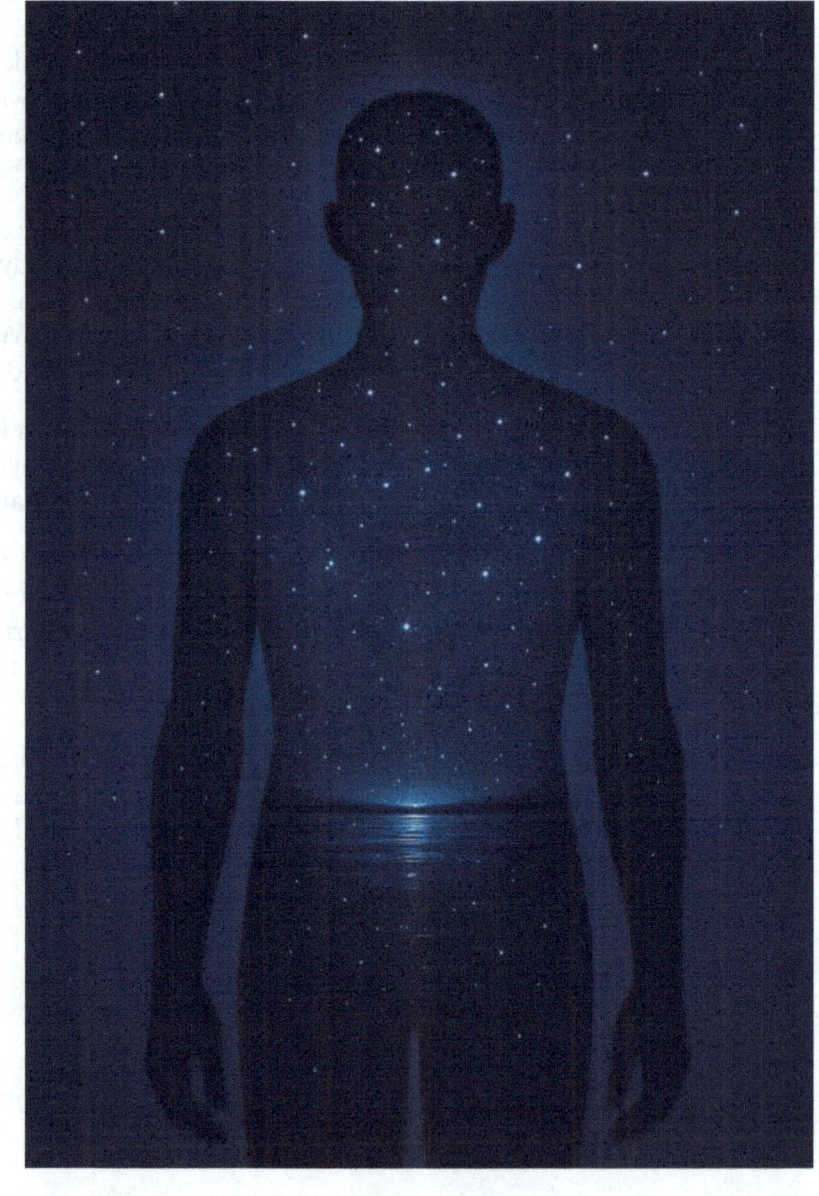

The body itself becomes the vessel of reflection. The eyes are twin stars, the breath a flowing tide, the spine a column linking earth and sky. Ancient mystics taught that the human being is a microcosm, a world in miniature, containing the laws of creation within their own flesh and spirit. The heart beats with lunar rhythms, expanding and contracting like the waxing and waning moon. The cycles of sleep and wake echo the sun's rising and setting. Hormonal tides follow the pull of planets, subtle yet undeniable. To understand yourself is to read the universe. To understand the universe is to recognize yourself.

The cosmic mirror also reveals that what you perceive in the heavens is not neutral. The arrangement of stars and planets is not simply an external architecture; it interacts with the soul as a language of resonance. Each constellation is an archetypal imprint, a living story woven into the collective psyche. When you gaze upon Orion, you are not just seeing stars, you are touching an ancient myth inscribed both in the sky and in the hidden chambers of your memory. The stars awaken what already lives within you. The mirror works in both directions: the sky reflects the soul, and the soul recognizes itself in the sky.

This principle also carries responsibility. If the outer world is mirrored within, then chaos and harmony in society are not detached phenomena, but extensions of the inner state of humanity. Storms in collective consciousness stir storms in the outer world, just as unresolved conflict in the individual clouds perception. Conversely, when one person attains clarity and inner peace, their reflection ripples outward, subtly reordering the field around them. The cosmic mirror is not passive, it is creative. It shows not only what is, but what may become when inner and outer are brought into harmony. Mystical traditions across cultures affirm this truth. In Vedic cosmology, the purusha, the cosmic person, is said to contain the universe in every limb. In Kabbalah, Adam Kadmon is envisioned as the primordial human whose body is the template of creation. In Hermetic thought, the human being is a star-bound reflection of the divine mind, containing both heaven and earth. The Native American traditions speak of walking in balance with the "star nation," seeing one's actions on earth as inseparably tied to celestial rhythms. All point to the same recognition: that the true temple is the human being, whose structure echoes the order of the cosmos.

To practice living with the cosmic mirror is to cultivate awareness that every gesture, thought, and breath is part of a universal rhythm. It is to awaken the sense of belonging that dissolves alienation and separation. When you feel overwhelmed by vastness, return to your breath: in it, the universe contracts into intimacy. When you feel confined by limitation, gaze at the stars: in them, the universe expands into endless possibility. Both movements are reflections of the same truth, above and within are one. The mirror also teaches humility. For as much as you carry the cosmos within, you are not its master. The reflection is not control but participation. The stars do not bend to your will, nor do you dissolve into them. Rather, you are a note in a vast harmony, unique yet inseparable from the whole. To live by the cosmic mirror is to listen for the music that binds opposites: the infinite and the finite, the universal and the personal, the above and the within. The mirror calls you into remembrance. Each star is not only a distant sun but a spark of your own light. Each constellation is not only a celestial pattern but a map of your inner journey. When you look upward, you are also looking inward. When you turn inward, you discover the heavens already shining. The veil between them dissolves in the still waters of the heart. There, the reflection becomes clear: the cosmos is not something you observe, it is what you are.

6.2 The Zodiac in Your Body

Ancient wisdom traditions consistently taught that the human being is not separate from the cosmos but a living microcosm reflecting the order of the heavens. Among the most striking illustrations of this principle is the doctrine of zodiacal correspondence, in which the twelve signs of the zodiac are mapped onto the human body from head to feet. This teaching, known in Hermetic, astrological, and mystical texts, proposes that each region of the body resonates with a specific zodiac sign, carrying its energy, symbolism, and influence. By understanding these correspondences, one begins to see the body not simply as a biological vessel but as a living star map, where cosmic rhythms and earthly embodiment converge. The system traditionally begins with Aries at the head. Aries, as the first sign of the zodiac, represents initiation, will, and fiery spark. Positioned at the head, it symbolizes thought, impulse, and the beginning of action. Ancient astrologers often described Aries as ruling the face, eyes, and brain, suggesting that the clarity or turbulence of one's mind can be tied to the vitality of this fiery archetype. The boldness of Aries energy, when balanced, becomes clarity of vision and decisive action. When blocked, it can manifest as headaches, tension, or impulsive mental restlessness.

Moving downward, Taurus governs the neck and throat. Associated with stability, beauty, and expression, Taurus embodies the power of voice. Singers, poets, and speakers have long been said to carry a Taurean resonance in their throats, where vibration and sound shape reality. The throat also symbolizes value and truth, since what one expresses reflects inner worth. Imbalances here might show as difficulty expressing oneself or throat-related ailments. The gift of Taurus is the capacity to speak or sing with grounded truth and to anchor the body in calm strength.

Gemini rules the shoulders, arms, and hands, reflecting its archetype of communication, dexterity, and duality. Just as Gemini connects ideas, the arms connect the center of the body to the world around it. The hands are instruments of writing, building, and creating, all acts of communication. The nervous system, also under Gemini's influence, shows the sign's association with swiftness and adaptability. When harmonious, Gemini fosters mental agility and skilled communication; when blocked, it can create scattered energy or nervous imbalance.

Cancer, symbolized by the nurturing crab, governs the chest and breasts. This placement highlights the themes of nourishment, care, and emotional protection. The chest houses the lungs and heart, where breath and life circulate. The breasts signify nourishment, aligning with Cancer's maternal symbolism. A balanced Cancerian energy in the chest allows for deep emotional attunement and the ability to give and receive love; an imbalance can manifest as shallow breathing, anxiety, or difficulty opening the heart.

Leo, the sign of the radiant lion, rules the heart and upper back. The heart is the throne of vitality, courage, and love, perfectly mirroring Leo's fiery rulership. Ancient texts spoke of the heart as the "sun within the body," radiating warmth and light to every cell. The back, supporting the chest, conveys dignity and pride. When Leo energy flows freely, it fuels generosity, confidence, and creativity. When hindered, it can collapse into arrogance, fear of rejection, or circulatory imbalances.

Virgo extends her influence over the abdomen, intestines, and digestive system. Known as the sign of service, refinement, and discernment, Virgo reflects the body's capacity to process, sort, and assimilate nourishment. The intestines, filtering and extracting what is useful, mirror Virgo's ability to analyze and distinguish. When Virgo's energy is honored, digestion flows smoothly, both physically and mentally; when unbalanced, issues such as worry, perfectionism, or digestive troubles may arise.

Libra, the sign of balance and relationship, governs the kidneys and lower back. The kidneys filter fluids, maintaining equilibrium, just as Libra seeks harmony in relationships and life. The lower back, structurally balancing the upper body, echoes Libra's archetype of fairness and support. In health, Libra's gift is the capacity to create beauty and justice. When challenged, imbalance may appear as indecision, dependence, or kidney-related ailments.

Scorpio rules the reproductive organs and processes of elimination. This placement reveals Scorpio's themes of transformation, intimacy, and regeneration. Just as the reproductive system brings forth life, Scorpio's power lies in creation and rebirth. Elimination signifies release, death, and renewal. Scorpio's energy, when harnessed, grants depth, passion, and healing; when shadowed, it may manifest as secrecy, obsession, or reproductive imbalances.

Sagittarius governs the hips, thighs, and movement. The thighs, carrying the body forward, symbolize exploration and expansion, perfectly mirroring Sagittarius's love of travel and higher knowledge. The hips, stabilizing the body, provide strength in forward motion. In balance, Sagittarius energy fuels freedom, optimism, and adventurous learning. In disharmony, it can create recklessness, restlessness, or tension in the hips and legs.

Capricorn rules the knees and skeletal structure. The knees allow one to bend and rise, reflecting Capricorn's lessons of humility, discipline, and endurance. The bones, providing the framework of the body, mirror Capricorn's structural nature in society and life. Balanced Capricorn energy yields resilience and mastery of form; when blocked, it may manifest as rigidity, fear of failure, or joint issues.

Aquarius governs the calves, ankles, and circulation. The ankles provide flexibility and direction, just as Aquarius provides innovation and new pathways. The calves propel movement, echoing Aquarius's forward-looking vision. Circulation, moving energy throughout the body, resonates with Aquarius's role in collective consciousness. Its gift is originality and humanitarian vision; its shadow is detachment, unpredictability, or circulatory imbalance.

Finally, Pisces rules the feet, the foundation and contact point with the earth. The feet carry the body, connecting it with the material world, while Pisces symbolizes transcendence and return to unity. The feet remind us that even spiritual beings must walk in the world. Harmonious Pisces energy nurtures compassion, intuition, and surrender; in disharmony, it may create escapism, confusion, or weakness in grounding.

Together, the zodiac mapped onto the body provides a holistic system of understanding. It reveals the body as a sacred instrument, tuned to cosmic harmonies, with each part resonating with archetypal energies of the heavens. By meditating on these correspondences, one can begin to embody astrology not merely as a tool of prediction but as a living dialogue between stars and flesh. The human body becomes not just a biological organism but a temple of the cosmos, a reminder that to know oneself is also to know the stars.

Zodiac Correspondences in the Human Body

Zodiac Sign	Body Part/Region	Spiritual Gift	Possible Imbalance
Aries	Head, face, brain, eyes	Initiation, clarity, vision, decisive action	Headaches, impulsivity, mental restlessness
Taurus	Neck, throat, voice	Expression of truth, stability, grounded creativity	Throat issues, blocked self-expression, stubbornness
Gemini	Shoulders, arms, hands, nervous system	Communication, dexterity, adaptability	Nervous tension, scattered thoughts, restlessness
Cancer	Chest, lungs, breasts	Nurturing, emotional attunement, receptivity	Anxiety, shallow breathing, difficulty receiving love
Leo	Heart, upper back, spine	Radiance, courage, creativity, generosity	Heart strain, pride, fear of rejection
Virgo	Abdomen, intestines, digestion	Discernment, refinement, integration	Digestive issues, worry, perfectionism
Libra	Kidneys, lower back	Harmony, fairness, relational balance	Indecision, dependency, kidney imbalances
Scorpio	Reproductive organs, elimination	Transformation, depth, intimacy, regeneration	Obsession, secrecy, reproductive or elimination issues
Sagittarius	Hips, thighs, mobility	Expansion, freedom, wisdom, exploration	Restlessness, recklessness, hip or thigh tension
Capricorn	Knees, bones, skeletal system	Endurance, structure, mastery	Rigidity, fear of failure, joint issues
Aquarius	Calves, ankles, circulation	Innovation, collective vision, adaptability	Detachment, unpredictability, circulatory problems
Pisces	Feet, grounding	Compassion, intuition, surrender, unity	Escapism, confusion, lack of grounding

6.3 Sacred Geometry of the Flesh

To look at the human body only as a cluster of bones, tissues, and nerves is to miss the deeper design that underlies its form. Across cultures, mystics, architects, and healers have recognized that the body is not random but is built upon timeless patterns of sacred geometry. These same ratios and forms shape galaxies, seashells, flowers, and even the orbits of planets. When we see the human body through this lens, we begin to understand ourselves as living mandalas, embodiments of universal order expressed in flesh.

One of the most striking correspondences is the golden ratio, also known as Phi, approximately 1.618. This ratio appears wherever life expresses harmony, efficiency, and beauty. In the human form, Phi manifests in countless ways: the relationship between the length of the forearm and the hand, between the segments of the fingers, between the height of the body and the position of the navel. Artists of the Renaissance used this proportion to idealize human figures, but it is not an invention of art. It is a discovery of what already exists in our living blueprint. When you stand upright, the distance from your head to your navel compared to the distance from your navel to your feet often approximates Phi. This proportion is nature's fingerprint written into your very stance.

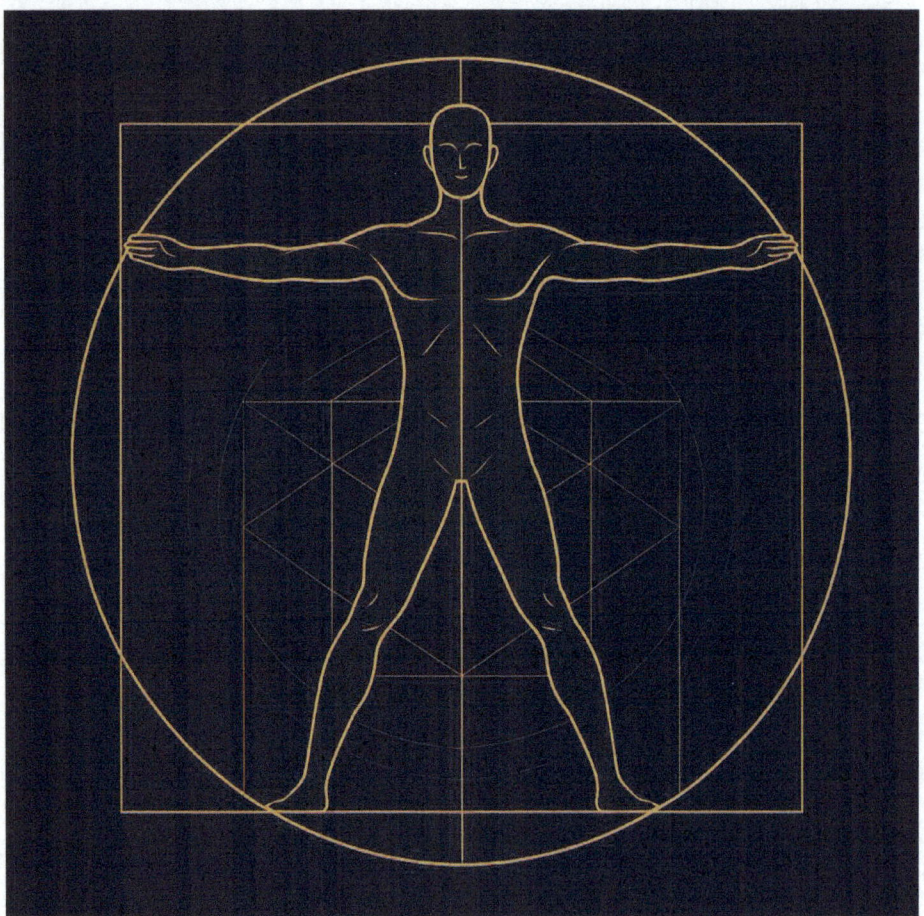

The spiral, derived from the golden ratio, is equally central. In seashells, hurricanes, and galaxies, the spiral carries the energy of growth and expansion. The body too follows this flow. Muscles coil, the cochlea of the ear spirals inward, DNA itself twists in a double helix. When a dancer spins, the body momentarily becomes a spiral in motion, mirroring the pattern of the universe. In meditation, some practitioners sense subtle currents rising in spiral-like flows through the spine, suggesting that our energy does not only move vertically but unfolds in rhythmic turns.

Beyond Phi and spirals, the geometric solids provide another lens of understanding. The Platonic solids, revered in ancient Greece, are five perfect shapes from which all matter was believed to arise. Each has been linked with an element: cube with earth, tetrahedron with fire, octahedron with air, icosahedron with water, and dodecahedron with ether. These forms can be overlaid upon the body to reveal deeper correspondences. The cube resonates with the solid structure of bones, while the icosahedron echoes the fluidity of blood and lymph. The dodecahedron, composed of twelve pentagons, is often associated with the higher etheric template of the human form, a subtle geometry guiding the visible body. Sacred geometry also maps onto the energy centers, sometimes called chakras or seals. Each center aligns with geometric patterns. The root resonates with the square or cube, symbol of stability. The sacral center connects to the crescent and circle, representing flow and generation. The heart is often shown as a hexagram or star, balancing above and below. The crown radiates as a circle of many petals, akin to an infinite lotus but also resonant with the dodecahedron's expansion into multidimensional space. These mappings are not arbitrary. They are visual languages to describe the symmetry and resonance perceived in states of heightened awareness.

Modern science too affirms aspects of these ancient insights. Studies in biomechanics reveal how spirals provide the most efficient distribution of force in tendons and fascia. The golden ratio is found in the branching of bronchial tubes and blood vessels. Even the heartbeat, when graphed, shows fractal patterns that echo natural geometry. While science tends to describe these as outcomes of evolutionary optimization, the contemplative traditions see them as signatures of cosmic intelligence. Both perspectives, though different in tone, point to the same truth: geometry is the language of life itself.

When we see sacred geometry in our bodies, our awareness changes. Every curve and pattern mirrors the cosmos, showing us we are part of an eternal design. To breathe with this awareness is to feel deep belonging, as a living equation of the universe.

This perspective can become practical in daily life. Visualizing the golden spiral moving through your spine while breathing can create a sense of spaciousness and flow. Meditating on the Flower of Life or Metatron's Cube overlaid on your body can awaken awareness of subtle alignments. Even standing in stillness and sensing the proportions between your body's parts can anchor you in harmony. These contemplations are not about intellectual analysis but about re-patterning perception so that the sacred is revealed in the ordinary. Sacred geometry also provides a way to bridge disciplines. Architects once designed cathedrals using the same ratios present in the body, believing that spaces built in resonance with human proportions would uplift the soul. Musicians tuned instruments to frequencies derived from these ratios, aligning sound with form. Healers visualized geometric lattices of light to restore balance in the body. Each field, whether art, music, or medicine, recognized that to align with geometry was to align with the fabric of creation.

To call the body a temple is more than a metaphor. Just as sacred buildings encode geometry, so does the human form. Entering awareness of the body can awaken the same awe as entering a cathedral. Flesh and spirit are not opposed but interwoven, and geometry reveals this union. To study it is not to reduce the body to lines, but to see it as a cosmic poem shaped in ratios and spirals. In the mirror, you are not just a face but an unfolding mandala, the very geometry through which the universe knows itself.

Chapter 7 – The Alchemy of Breath and Water

7.1 Breath as Prayer

7.1.1 The First and Last Breath

The story of human life is written between two breaths. The moment a newborn emerges into the world, the cry that fills its lungs is both fragile and thunderous, declaring the presence of a new soul. From that first inhalation, the body begins a rhythm that continues without pause, shaping every moment of earthly existence. At the other end of the journey, the final exhalation carries the weight of release, marking the soul's passage beyond the veil. Breath frames the beginning and end of human embodiment, and for this reason, across traditions and philosophies, it has always been understood as sacred.

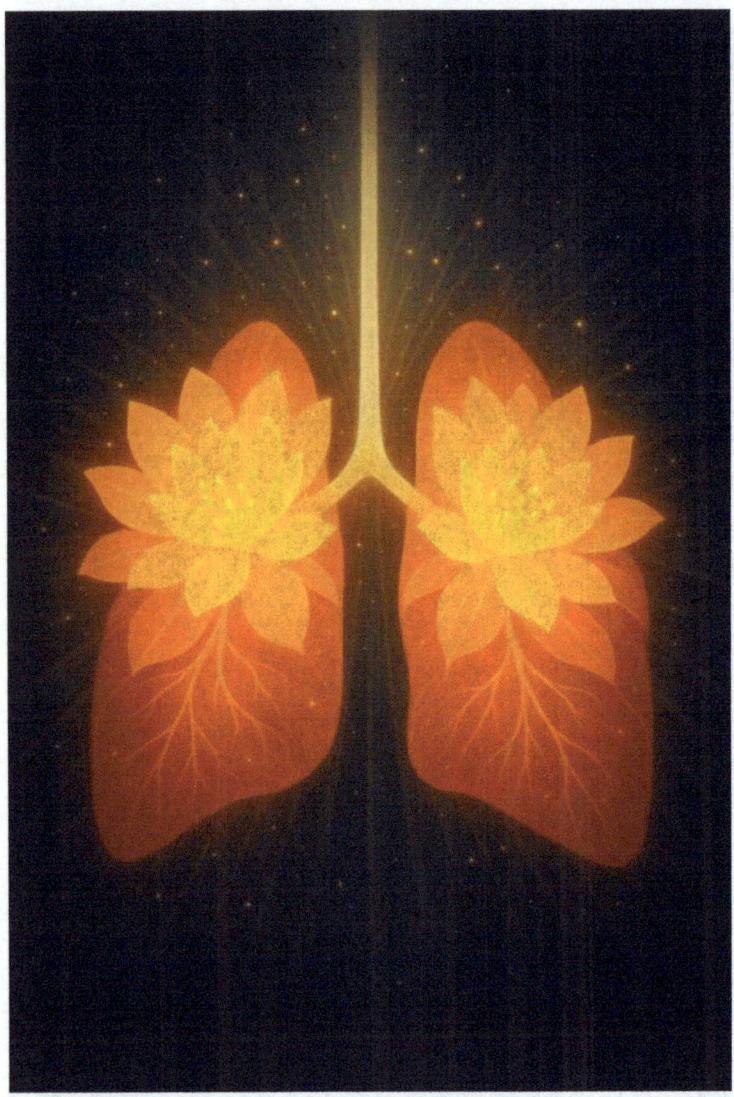

In Greek thought, the word *pneuma* means both breath and spirit, a reminder that the invisible current that sustains the body is also what animates consciousness. In Sanskrit, the term *prana* carries a similar resonance, describing the life-force that flows through all beings, entering with the inhale and circulating through subtle channels within the body. In Hebrew, the word *ruach* is both wind and divine spirit, the breath of God moving across creation. These linguistic echoes reveal a deep and universal recognition: to breathe is to participate in the presence of spirit, and the rhythm of respiration is the most intimate dialogue between the body and the infinite.

When a child first draws air, it is not merely oxygen that fills the lungs. The act of breathing is a claim upon existence. The lungs unfold like wings that had been dormant, hidden until the moment of arrival. This is why so many traditions view the first breath as the entry of the soul into earthly form. In certain Indigenous perspectives, elders describe the newborn's first cry as a signal to the ancestors that a new traveler has joined the human family. It is the audible seal of incarnation.

Between the first and last breath stretches the vast tapestry of living, each inhalation and exhalation weaving the fabric of memory, emotion, and experience. Most of the time, breath goes unnoticed, flowing in the background like a silent river. Yet the ancients understood that this current is not passive. It reflects the state of the inner being. Shallow breath reveals fear or unrest, while slow, steady breathing shows balance and presence. Every tradition that speaks of spirit through breath emphasizes this mirror-like quality. The way a person breathes is the way they live.

At the end of life, when the last breath departs, silence follows. Those who have witnessed a loved one's passing often describe the moment as both devastating and profoundly holy. The breath that once tied body to world has been released, and something intangible but unmistakable has gone. Here lies the reason breath is called sacred across cultures: it does not simply sustain the body, it is the bridge between the seen and unseen, the finite and infinite.

In Christian scripture, the very creation of humanity is described through divine breath. "God breathed into Adam's nostrils the breath of life, and he became a living soul." In Hindu philosophy, the cosmos itself expands and contracts with the breathing of Brahman, suggesting that human respiration is a reflection of cosmic rhythm. In Islamic mysticism, the *Nafas al-Rahman*, the Breath of the Merciful, is the sustaining presence of God that holds all creation in being. Across cultures, breath is not only physiology but theology, not only a function of the body but a revelation of the spirit.

The sacredness of the final exhalation has also inspired rituals of passage. In Tibetan Buddhism, practitioners are trained to recognize the dissolution of breath as a gateway into luminous awareness, using death as an initiation rather than an end. In many Christian traditions, prayers accompany the dying so that the soul may be carried on the breath of God into eternity. In ancient Egypt, texts describe the deceased breathing in divine air as they awaken to the afterlife. These diverse visions share a common root: breath belongs not solely to the individual, but to a greater field of spirit that continues when the body ceases. Because breath is both universal and personal, it is one of the few experiences that links all of humanity without exception. Every person alive right now, across the globe, shares this rhythm. The poor and the wealthy, the strong and the frail, the old and the young, all are bound by the same invisible tide. This is why sages often taught that awareness of breath can awaken compassion. To recognize that another is breathing is to remember that they are as alive, vulnerable, and sacred as oneself.

From the first cry to the last sigh, breath is a teacher. It reminds us of impermanence, of the gift of each moment, and of the presence of spirit hidden in the simplest act. To pause and feel the air moving in and out is to touch the very mystery of life. This is why breath has been described as prayer without words: every inhale is an offering of presence, every exhale a surrender into trust. The first breath opens the door into form, the last breath opens the door beyond form, and in between, the soul learns the art of being.

7.1.2 Breath and Spirit Across Traditions

Breath has always been more than a biological necessity. Across civilizations and faiths, it has been seen as the direct current of spirit, the hidden thread binding flesh to soul. The rhythm of inhalation and exhalation is so constant that it is easy to overlook, yet traditions from the East to the West recognized breath as a sacred key, a subtle force that bridges the visible and the invisible. When you study how cultures named and revered it, you begin to see a striking universality: breath is not just oxygen and carbon dioxide, but life's very spark.

In Greek thought, the word *pneuma* carried a layered meaning. It denoted breath, wind, and spirit all at once. To breathe was to participate in the cosmic wind that moved the heavens. Stoic philosophers described pneuma as the animating principle that pervades the world, giving coherence to matter. When early Christians spoke of the Holy Spirit, they used this same word, emphasizing that divine presence was experienced as a breath moving through the believer. In this way, pneuma linked physiology, cosmology, and divinity, suggesting that each breath taken was also a quiet communion with the source of being.

The Hebrew scriptures preserved another profound vision of breath through the word *ruach*. In Hebrew, ruach means both wind and spirit. The opening verses of Genesis speak of the ruach of God moving upon the waters before creation unfolded. This was not merely air or weather, but the dynamic presence of life-force itself. Later prophets described God breathing life into humankind, filling dust with ruach to make it a living soul. In Jewish mysticism, this breath was understood as the subtle current of divine energy sustaining creation in every moment, without which existence would collapse back into silence. To breathe consciously, then, was to remember that one's life was not self-sustained but continually infused by divine generosity.

In Sanskrit traditions, the equivalent word was *prana*. While commonly translated as breath, prana was understood as a universal vital energy, moving through the channels of the body and connecting the individual to the wider cosmos. Yogic practices developed detailed methods for directing this life force through pranayama, or breath discipline. Each controlled inhalation and exhalation was not just exercise but alignment, balancing the inner winds so that the practitioner could attune body, mind, and spirit to higher states of awareness. In this framework, prana was not confined to humans but circulated through animals, plants, rivers, even stones. Breathing with intention was thus a way of recognizing one's participation in the entire living web of existence.

In China, the concept of *qi* (sometimes written *chi*) offered another perspective on breath. Qi was described as the subtle breath of life that circulates through the meridians of the body, animating organs and shaping health. In Taoist texts, qi also filled valleys, flowed in rivers, and moved with the wind across the mountains. Breathing practices in qigong and Taoist meditation were designed to refine and gather qi, allowing the adept to harmonize with the rhythms of the cosmos. To breathe deeply was not merely to oxygenate blood, but to enter into resonance with the pulse of the Tao itself. Even martial arts embedded this principle, teaching that mastery of breath meant mastery of energy, balance, and power.

Indigenous cultures across the Americas also held breath as sacred. Among some Native traditions, breath was considered the personal spirit of a being, a breath-gift given by Creator. To speak or sing was to release part of that spirit into the world, shaping reality through the vibration of words. Ceremonial practices often included intentional breathing, smoke, or wind as visible signs of the invisible current that connects all life. Among the Navajo, the Holy Wind was said to inhabit every person, moving within the body and linking them to the great order of existence. Breath here was inseparable from identity, relationship, and destiny.

The ancient Egyptians developed another rich symbolism through the word *ka*, often translated as the vital essence or breath of life. Depictions of gods creating humans show them holding the ankh, the symbol of life, to the nose of the new being, as if transmitting the sacred breath directly. The ka was believed to accompany a person throughout life and even into the afterlife, nourished by offerings and prayers. To sustain the ka was to sustain the individual's spiritual presence, demonstrating once more that breath was understood as the carrier of continuity between worlds.

Even in modern science, echoes of these insights remain. The autonomic nervous system links breath to states of consciousness, demonstrating physiologically what mystics taught symbolically: slow, deep breathing calms the mind and restores balance, while rapid or shallow breathing agitates the system.

Neuroscience now confirms that patterns of breath influence brainwaves, emotional regulation, and even immune response. Though science uses different language, it recognizes breath as a regulator of life far deeper than mere gas exchange. It shapes experience, perception, and resilience.

When we gather these traditions, a remarkable pattern emerges. Whether named pneuma, ruach, prana, qi, or ka, breath is consistently described as the medium of spirit. It is the invisible that animates the visible, the unifying current between body and cosmos. What seems ordinary and mechanical is in fact a sacred exchange, a ceaseless communion. This recognition is not limited to any single culture, but woven across humanity like a hidden script.

To practice awareness of breath, then, is not simply to calm stress or focus attention, though those benefits are real. It is to enter into the same mystery that sages, prophets, and healers have contemplated for millennia. Each inhalation becomes a reception of life's generosity, each exhalation a return of that gift back into the world. Breathing with reverence awakens the realization that one is never isolated, never truly alone. The same breath moving through you now is the breath that moved across the waters of creation, the breath that whispered to prophets, the breath that filled temples with song. To remember this is to live differently, for breath reveals that life itself is prayer, continuous and unbroken.

7.1.3 Practices of Breath-Offering

Every tradition has carried the secret that your breath can become more than a biological rhythm. It can be a prayer, a key, an offering to the Source. When you shift from unconscious breathing to intentional breath-offering, every inhale and exhale becomes a dialogue with the divine blueprint encoded in your being.

The practice begins with remembering that breath is light in motion. When you inhale, imagine drawing not only air but streams of luminous presence entering through your nostrils, cascading down into your chest, and expanding within your lungs. With each expansion you are not just filling tissue, you are opening the temple within. As you hold that breath gently for a moment, sense it glowing in the center of your heart like a lamp being kindled.

Then comes the exhale, the act of release. But here it becomes more than just carbon leaving the body. Each exhale becomes prayer. You breathe out with intention, shaping the air into a message. It does not have to be words, though you may whisper if you choose. The exhale itself is a vibration of offering, a release of gratitude, forgiveness, or devotion. Some breathe out silently "thank you," others simply exhale light. What matters is that you know the breath leaving you is carrying your heart back into the field of Spirit.

A simple daily ritual unfolds in three movements:

1. **Breathing in Light** – Sit quietly, spine tall, eyes closed. Imagine the universe pouring golden light into you with every inhale. Breathe slowly, deeply, and let that light enter not only your lungs but your bones, your bloodstream, even your thoughts.

2. **Holding as Flame** – At the top of the inhale, pause. Visualize the light as a radiant flame at the center of your chest, steady and alive. This pause is sacred. It is the place of recognition, where breath and soul meet.

3. **Exhaling as Prayer** – Release the breath gently, with awareness. Imagine it flowing outward not only from your lungs but from your entire being, carrying an offering of love, peace, or blessing to the world around you. If you wish, silently form a word such as "peace," "love," or "light" and breathe it into existence.

Practiced daily, even for five minutes, this ritual rewrites how you experience both breath and life. You begin to feel that you are not only inhaling oxygen but receiving direct transmission from Source. You are not only exhaling waste but sending currents of prayer into the fabric of reality.

Over time, the breath becomes an altar. Every inhale is an anointing, every exhale a psalm. You walk through the day breathing not only for survival but for communion. And when you live like this, you realize that prayer is no longer something you perform at certain hours. It is as close as the next breath, already waiting, already sacred.

7.2 Water Memory

7.2.1 The Living Intelligence of Water

Water is the most ordinary substance in your daily life, and yet it hides the most extraordinary mystery. You drink it, wash with it, bathe in it, and never question its silence. But water listens. Water remembers. Water responds. The ancients already knew this truth, and now modern experiments are beginning to confirm what myth and ritual preserved for thousands of years.

One of the most well-known explorations of water's hidden sensitivity came through the experiments of

Masaru Emoto. In his studies, water samples were exposed to words, prayers, music, and even thoughts. When frozen and examined under a microscope, the crystalline structures revealed a startling pattern. Water blessed with loving words formed symmetrical, radiant snowflake-like crystals. Water subjected to hateful words or harsh vibrations revealed distorted, broken, or incomplete forms. Whether or not one accepts every detail of his research, the images themselves awaken an intuition: water reflects the vibration it receives.

Why does this matter? Because water makes up most of your body. Each cell is bathed in fluid, and your bloodstream, your lymph, your very tears are rivers of remembrance. If water outside of you responds to intention, how much more does the water within you resonate with the quality of your thoughts, your emotions, your prayers. When you speak gently to yourself, you are literally reshaping the crystalline structure of your being. When you live in gratitude, the rivers in your blood harmonize.

Ancient cultures treated water not as a resource but as a living intelligence. The Nile, the Ganges, the Jordan, the springs of Delphi, the wells of Celtic groves, all were considered portals to the divine. Water was not only life but spirit in motion. The Greek philosopher Thales named water as the primal element from which all life arises. In the Hebrew scriptures, the Spirit of God hovers over the waters before creation begins. In the Quran, it is said that every living thing is made from water. To drink water was never just hydration—it was communion with the Source.

Even science is beginning to whisper similar truths. Research into water's molecular structure suggests that it can form clusters that shift in response to environment, light, and energy fields. Some propose that these clusters hold "memory," capable of being imprinted with subtle information. This does not reduce water to a mere medium but elevates it to the role of messenger. Water may be the bridge between the material and the immaterial, carrying intention into form.

Think of your own relationship with water. You shower to cleanse, you drink to survive, you may sit by a river to find peace. But if you shift perspective, you may begin to sense that the water is not passive in this exchange. It receives your tension and washes it away. It enters your mouth and carries vitality into your cells. It laps against the shore as if whispering something you forgot. To engage water consciously is to step back into the covenant humans once held with the natural world.

What happens when you bless your glass of water before drinking? When you whisper "thank you" before pouring tea? When you hold a bottle of water and visualize it filling with light? You are not performing a superstition, you are participating in the dialogue of creation. You are acknowledging that matter and spirit are not separate. You are remembering that water is alive.

The living intelligence of water means that every drop you encounter is also a mirror. It reflects back your state of being. It teaches you that clarity comes from purity, that turbulence distorts reflection, that stillness reveals hidden depth. When you truly understand this, every sip becomes prayer, every river a teacher, every rainfall a baptism. You begin to realize that the same intelligence flowing through rivers and oceans is flowing through you.

This is why water is sacred across so many cultures, and why every ritual of cleansing, blessing, and renewal finds its way back to this element. Water is not only what sustains you, it is what listens to you, remembers you, and shapes you. To forget this is to live in exile. To remember it is to return to the stream of wisdom that has always been flowing.

7.2.2 Traditions of Sacred Waters

Water has always been more than a physical substance. Across cultures and centuries, it has been revered as a bridge between the visible and invisible, the material and the divine. Sacred waters are not simply about physical cleansing, they symbolize rebirth, renewal, and alignment with the eternal flow of creation. By entering or consuming consecrated water, individuals step into a larger spiritual current that binds body, mind, and soul to something greater.

In Christianity, baptism represents one of the clearest expressions of this truth. Immersion or sprinkling with water marks the beginning of a new spiritual life. The act echoes death and resurrection, an immersion into the grave of the old self and a rising into renewed identity. The waters of baptism are not ordinary, they are believed to be infused with divine grace, transforming them into a portal through which one enters communion with the Spirit. What may appear as a ritual bath is actually a profound initiation into sacred belonging.

Judaism preserves a parallel expression through the practice of the mikveh, a ritual bath used for purification. The mikveh is not just about hygiene, it signifies restoration of wholeness and readiness to encounter the holy. Whether after childbirth, before marriage, or to mark spiritual renewal, immersion in the mikveh reconnects the individual to the flowing rhythm of creation. Jewish mystics describe water as an element that dissolves boundaries, returning the soul to a primordial state of purity. Entering the mikveh is like returning to the womb of divine presence and emerging reborn.

In Hinduism, the waters of the Ganga River hold legendary power. Millions of pilgrims travel to its banks to bathe, believing that contact with the Ganga cleanses karmic burdens and accelerates spiritual liberation. The Ganga is not merely a river, it is a goddess, a living embodiment of divine grace flowing through the world. To immerse in her waters is to touch eternity, to be carried in the stream of divine compassion. This reverence demonstrates how water becomes both an earthly substance and a celestial being, existing simultaneously in both worlds.

The Shinto tradition in Japan embraces a similar reverence in the practice of misogi, a ritual of purification by standing beneath waterfalls or immersing in cold rivers. Practitioners do not see the water as ordinary, but as a conduit of divine presence that cleanses the spiritual body. The shock of cold is understood as an awakening, breaking through dullness and washing away stagnant energies. Misogi is not just ritual, it is a dialogue with the kami, the divine spirits of nature, through the living flow of water.

Though these traditions come from different continents and different epochs, they reveal a common pattern. Sacred waters are never passive, they are alive, intelligent, and transformative. They act

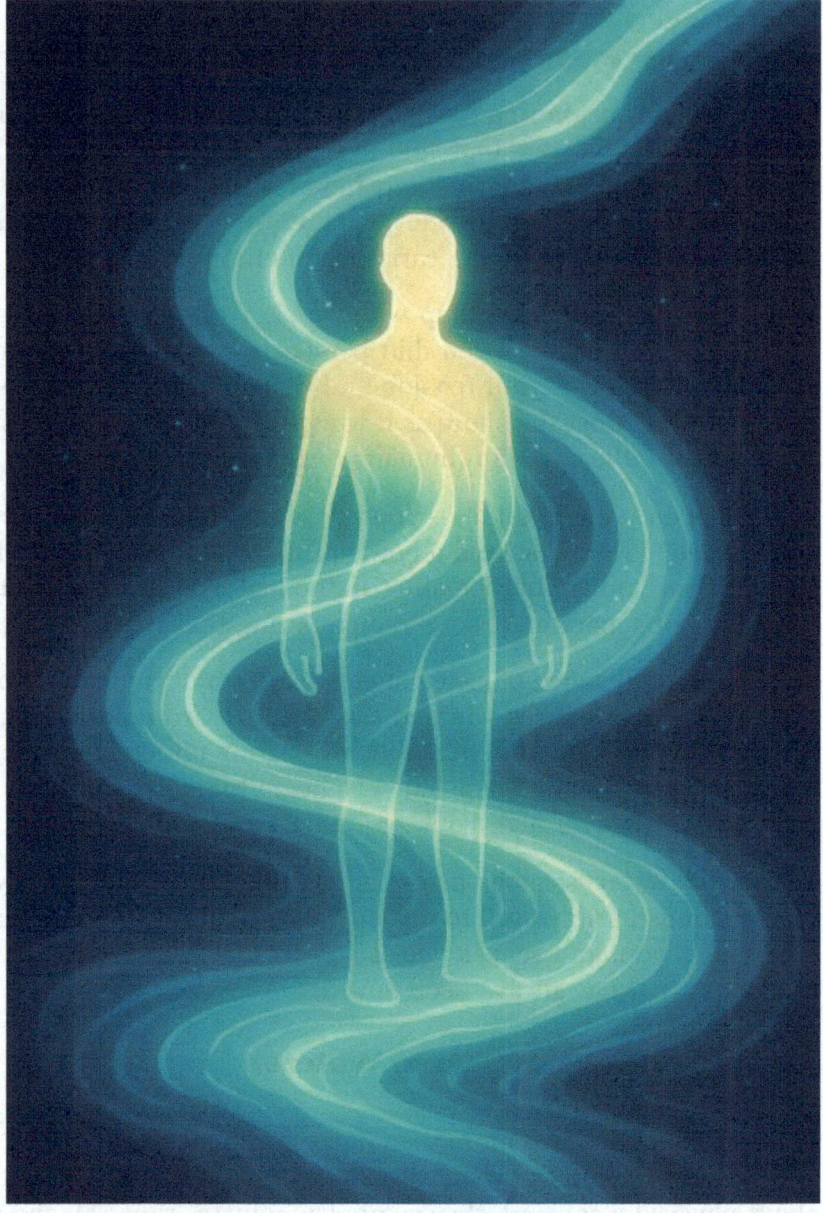

as mirrors that reflect both the outer act and the inner state. When one steps into baptismal waters, a mikveh, the Ganga, or beneath a Shinto waterfall, the physical body may touch water, but the soul is immersed in light. This universality hints that humanity, regardless of culture, has always recognized water as more than chemistry, but as the carrier of spirit.

For the seeker today, these traditions offer an invitation. Water is not just for quenching thirst or washing away dust. It can become a daily sacrament if approached with reverence. Even a glass drawn from the tap can serve as a vessel of transformation if one approaches it with the same intention as pilgrims by the Ganga or initiates in the mikveh. To drink water mindfully, to bless it, to see it as a living presence, is to rediscover what these traditions have guarded for millennia: that water remembers, carries, and conveys the eternal.

Sacred waters teach us that spirituality is not confined to the heavens. It flows around us and through us in the simplest and most essential of elements. Every time you wash, bathe, or drink, you touch an ancient current that countless souls before you have entered. The rivers of the earth are rivers of the spirit, and when you step into them, you step into the timeless stream of the sacred.

Comparative Chart of "Water as Sacred in Different Traditions"

Tradition	Symbol / Practice	Meaning and Function
Christianity	Baptism	Entry into spiritual life, cleansing of sin, rebirth in Christ.
Judaism	Mikveh (ritual bath)	Purification, spiritual renewal, preparation for sacred acts.
Hinduism	Ganga River	Sacred river embodying divine mother, believed to wash away karma.
Shinto (Japan)	Misogi (water purification)	Ritual cleansing of body and spirit, restoring harmony with kami.
Islam	Wudu and Ghusl	Ablutions with water before prayer, symbolizing purity and readiness.
Indigenous Traditions	Sacred springs, water offerings	Honoring water spirits, acknowledging water as life-giver and healer.

7.2.3 Contemplation: Drinking with Intention

Water is more than a physical necessity. It is a vessel, a messenger, and a bridge between the visible and invisible. When approached with intention, drinking becomes more than hydration, it becomes communion. This simple practice transforms an ordinary act into a daily ritual of alignment.

Begin by choosing your water with mindfulness. Whether it is spring water, filtered water, or even tap water, hold it with reverence. Recognize that this liquid has traveled rivers, clouds, and stones before reaching your hands. In your awareness, it becomes living, not inert.

Step one is blessing. Before drinking, place your hands around the glass. Breathe slowly, and speak a word of gratitude aloud or silently. You may say, "Thank you for life," or simply whisper your own prayer. Ancient traditions remind us that spoken intention impresses itself upon water's molecular memory, as experiments suggest, creating harmony within its structure.

Step two is imprinting. After blessing, visualize the water glowing softly in your cup. Imagine streams of light descending into it, carrying your intention. Perhaps it is clarity for the mind, calm for the heart, or renewal for the body. Envision that each droplet carries this message into your cells. In this moment, water is no longer neutral, it has become consecrated.

Step three is drinking mindfully. Lift the glass slowly and take a small sip. As it enters your mouth, pause. Feel the coolness, the texture, the taste. As you swallow, sense it traveling downward, moving into the body with purpose. Imagine it carrying your prayer into every cell, blessing your inner rivers, nourishing your blood, and renewing your organs.

Repeat sip by sip until the glass is empty. Close with a breath of gratitude. Even a few moments of silence after finishing can seal the practice.

This contemplation requires no elaborate ritual. It can be performed at home, in the workplace, or while traveling. Over time, the practice reshapes your relationship with the ordinary. Each glass of water becomes a prayer, a covenant, and a reminder of the intelligence flowing within you and around you.

When performed consistently, drinking with intention softens the boundaries between body and spirit. You realize that life itself is constantly being blessed, imprinted, and absorbed. Water becomes a teacher, showing that with awareness, even the simplest act is a portal to transformation.

7.3 The Inner Baptism

7.3.1 Light Cascading as Water

There are moments in the spiritual path when words fail, when images alone carry the weight of truth. Among the most enduring of these images is the vision of light descending like water, washing over and through the seeker until every fragment of heaviness is dissolved. This is not metaphor alone, it is a mystical reality described across traditions, where inner rebirth is experienced not through doctrine but through immersion in luminous waters.

To understand this vision, imagine yourself seated in stillness. The breath slows, the mind quiets, and a subtle awareness arises, like the calm before dawn. Then, as though a hidden veil parts above your head,

streams of radiance begin to pour down. It is not harsh or blinding, but soft, fluid, and alive. The light moves like water, cascading with a rhythm, surrounding you in its descent. It touches your head, your shoulders, and flows over your entire body until you are immersed in a silent waterfall of brilliance.

Mystics from every lineage have described this inner baptism. Early Christians spoke of the Spirit descending "as tongues of flame," yet others felt it as luminous water flooding the soul. Sufi poets describe being drowned in the ocean of divine light, while Hindu yogis speak of amrita, the nectar of immortality, dripping from the crown into the body. In Buddhism, meditative visions often depict cascades of radiance pouring through the channels of the subtle body. Though the imagery differs, the essence remains the same: an infusion of living light that cleanses, renews, and awakens.

This experience is not only visionary. It is deeply felt within the body. As the luminous waters flow, they carry away residue that the ordinary self cannot touch. Old memories, emotional burdens, the shadows of fear, and the fatigue of years begin to dissolve. What remains is an unmistakable freshness, as though the seeker has been born anew. The soul feels lighter, the body feels transparent, and the mind feels clear.

One reason light is often described as water is because both elements share qualities of renewal. Water cleanses, purifies, and sustains life. Light illuminates, heals, and awakens growth. When united in this mystical imagery, they convey the fullness of transformation: an external washing and an internal ignition. This double symbolism explains why so many initiatory rites on Earth employ water as the outward symbol of an inner illumination.

But unlike outward rites that depend on rivers, fonts, or ceremonies, the inner baptism requires no external source. The fountain is already within. When the crown of the head opens in reverence, when the heart is willing to receive, the descent begins naturally. It is as if the soul has finally aligned with the eternal current always flowing from the divine. You discover that you were never dry, only unaware of the waters pouring through you all along.

In this light-water descent, rebirth does not mean discarding the old self as something foreign. Instead, it means remembering the original purity that has always been hidden beneath the layers of experience. The flow does not make you into something new, it restores you to what you truly are. Every drop reminds you that you are not separate from the Source but continuously sustained by it.

Many who undergo this inner baptism describe a profound shift in identity. The world appears brighter, not because it has changed, but because their vision has been cleansed. Relationships feel lighter because the heaviness they carried no longer defines them. Even the breath feels different, as if each inhale carries light and each exhale releases burdens. It is not a momentary vision but an initiation into a new way of being.

To cultivate this experience, seekers often enter meditation with a clear intention: "I open to the descent of light." The practice is not one of effort but of surrender, like standing beneath a waterfall and simply allowing. The imagination assists at first, visualizing streams of radiance pouring down. Yet over time, the vision gives way to sensation. The crown tingles, the spine vibrates, and warmth or coolness floods the body. Slowly, what began as imagination becomes unmistakable presence.

This is why mystics call it a rebirth. For to be bathed in light-water is to remember that life is not merely survival or striving, but a gift continually renewed. Each descent is a reminder that you are not alone, not abandoned, but always immersed in a current of grace. The waters may seem to come from above, but in truth they emerge from within, where the soul and the infinite meet.

The inner baptism cannot be forced, yet it can be welcomed. Each act of stillness, each breath of surrender, each prayer of openness is like turning your face upward to receive the cascade. And when it comes, there is no mistaking it. You are not cleansed by metaphor, but by reality. You are washed by the luminous waters of eternity, and you emerge radiant, whole, and profoundly alive.

7.3.2 Fire and Water Within

The ancients spoke of fire and water not only as primal elements of the world, but as living archetypes dwelling in the soul. Fire was the spark of will, passion, and transformation, while water was the current of surrender, receptivity, and renewal. To understand the alchemy of the inner life, one must learn how these two seemingly opposing forces dance together rather than fight for dominance. In that balance lies inner mastery.

Fire rises, consuming and illuminating. It is the principle that drives you forward when you commit to a path, the determination that pushes through resistance, the inner flame that declares, "I am." Without fire, there is no clarity of direction, no ignition of vision, no courage to break through inertia. Yet left unchecked, fire burns without measure. It scorches relationships, dries up compassion, and leaves the inner ground cracked. This is why the wisdom traditions always paired it with water, teaching that fire must be contained within the vessel of humility and tenderness.

Water descends, enfolding and softening. It cleanses and restores, reminding you of the art of letting go. It is the principle of yielding without losing strength, of absorbing and flowing around obstacles rather than shattering against them. Without water, there is no nourishment of roots, no receptivity to higher guidance, no ability to bend without breaking. Yet if water dominates without balance, it drowns initiative, erodes willpower, and creates stagnation where movement should be.

The mystics knew that a soul entirely in fire is restless and unstable, while a soul entirely in water dissolves and loses shape. But when these two elements are held together in the heart, a third reality is born: harmony. This harmony is not achieved by muting either force but by allowing each to shine in its place. Fire is will, water is surrender, and together they create the paradoxical power to act with intensity while remaining aligned with the flow of life.

Alchemy described this as the marriage of opposites. In the furnace of the spirit, the flame of intention burns brightly, yet it does not consume because the waters of grace temper it. In many traditions, rituals of initiation symbolized this union. Baptisms were performed with water while prayers invoked the descent of fire. The Pentecost narrative in Christianity, where tongues of flame rest upon the disciples after immersion in water, is an echo of this elemental balance. In yogic practice, the kundalini is often described as a coiled fire rising, but its ascent must be cooled and guided by the lunar, watery currents of the subtle body.

The heart is the true meeting ground of fire and water. Imagine it as a chalice: within it burns a steady flame, the light of your purpose. Around it flows a gentle stream, ensuring that the fire never rages uncontrolled but also never extinguishes. This inner image reveals a secret: power does not come from domination of one element over the other, but from their sacred marriage.

In everyday life, this balance appears in simple but profound ways. When you pursue a goal with clarity yet are willing to adapt when life redirects you, you are embodying fire and water. When you speak with passion but allow your words to be softened with compassion, you are embodying fire and water. When you pray with fervent desire but release attachment to how it will manifest, you are embodying fire and water.

The imbalance is easy to recognize. If you find yourself driven, restless, and impatient, your fire may be untethered. If you find yourself passive, avoidant, and lacking will, your waters may have overflowed. The inner art is to invite what is lacking until the two flow together. Breath practices, for instance, can become a ritual of this harmonization: inhalation as the fire that rises, exhalation as the water that descends.

Mystics taught that the ultimate alchemy of the soul is not choosing between elements but letting them dance. Fire without water is tyranny of the will. Water without fire is surrender without form. But when the flame of your intention glows within the river of your surrender, you embody the paradox of strength and softness, clarity and compassion, will and trust. This paradox is the sign of maturity in the path.

In meditation, you may visualize this union within your own heart. See a small flame glowing steadily, not flickering wildly, representing your inner will. Around it, sense a soft current of water encircling, cooling, and embracing the flame. Notice how neither extinguishes the other but together form a radiant core. This is your inner temple, the sacred space where the two primal elements of creation rest in harmony.

When you live with this awareness, you no longer fear your intensity nor mistrust your softness. You become whole, and in that wholeness, the fire of will and the water of surrender cease to be opposites. They become the two wings of the same soul, carrying you into the deeper mysteries of life.

7.3.3 Practice: The Inner Anointing

Close your eyes and sit in stillness. Let your body find a position where breath flows easily and nothing feels forced. Imagine a subtle stream of luminous water descending from above, as if the heavens themselves are pouring a river of living light upon you. This is not ordinary water. It is water woven with light, carrying intelligence, cleansing memory, and restoring the original radiance within you.

Begin by bringing awareness to the crown of your head. See, feel, or simply sense a gentle cascade entering through this gateway. Let it touch the top of your skull like the first drops of rain, cool and tender. With each inhale, draw this light-water into your body. With each exhale, release the weight of old stories, stale emotions, and heavy impressions that no longer belong to you.

Now let the stream move downward. As it passes through your forehead, imagine it clearing away fog, confusion, and mental noise. A soft clarity begins to glow where once there was strain. At your throat, the waters swirl and open the channel of expression. Feel words unsaid and truths withheld dissolving in the current, leaving only the pure capacity to speak with integrity.

The stream continues to your heart. Here, pause and breathe deeply. Let the light-water pool inside your chest, washing away grief, resentment, and the ache of disappointments. Sense how the waters polish the heart like a stone in a riverbed, leaving it smooth, luminous, and open.

Draw the flow further down. At the solar plexus, it cools the fire of tension, dissolving fear of control or inadequacy. At the sacral center, it brings balance to desire, restoring a sense of creative innocence. At the root, it anchors you into the earth, leaving you both cleansed and grounded, connected to life itself.

Now visualize your whole body immersed in this river of light. It is not just falling upon you but rising from beneath, surrounding you entirely. You are seated inside a column of luminous water, endlessly flowing. Allow yourself to rest here. Notice the sensation of renewal, of inner baptism, of becoming clear and whole once more.

When you are ready, imagine the stream becoming gentler, fading into a soft mist. Feel gratitude for this inner anointing, as if you have been prepared for a new chapter of being. Slowly open your eyes, carrying the freshness of this practice with you.

The Inner Anointing is not a ritual for a special moment. It can be entered in a few breaths whenever you feel the need to release and reset. The more often you allow the light-water to cleanse you, the more natural it becomes to live as one continuously renewed.

Chapter 8 – The Hidden Organs of Perception

8.1 The Pineal Gate

Hidden deep within the brain, no larger than a grain of rice, rests the pineal gland. For centuries mystics and sages have referred to it as the "seat of the soul," the inner eye, the crystal gate between the visible and the invisible. Though medicine describes it as a regulator of circadian rhythms, ancient traditions saw it as a luminous portal of perception, awakening when consciousness is attuned to higher frequencies.

When you close your eyes in meditation, a darkness spreads before you. Yet within that darkness can arise a subtle glow, a sense of inner vision beyond physical sight. That glow, many mystics taught, is the pineal responding, flickering like a lamp that can illuminate the inner world. To contemplate the pineal gland is to recognize that perception is not confined to the eyes or ears but includes an inner sense, capable of discerning truth beyond appearances.

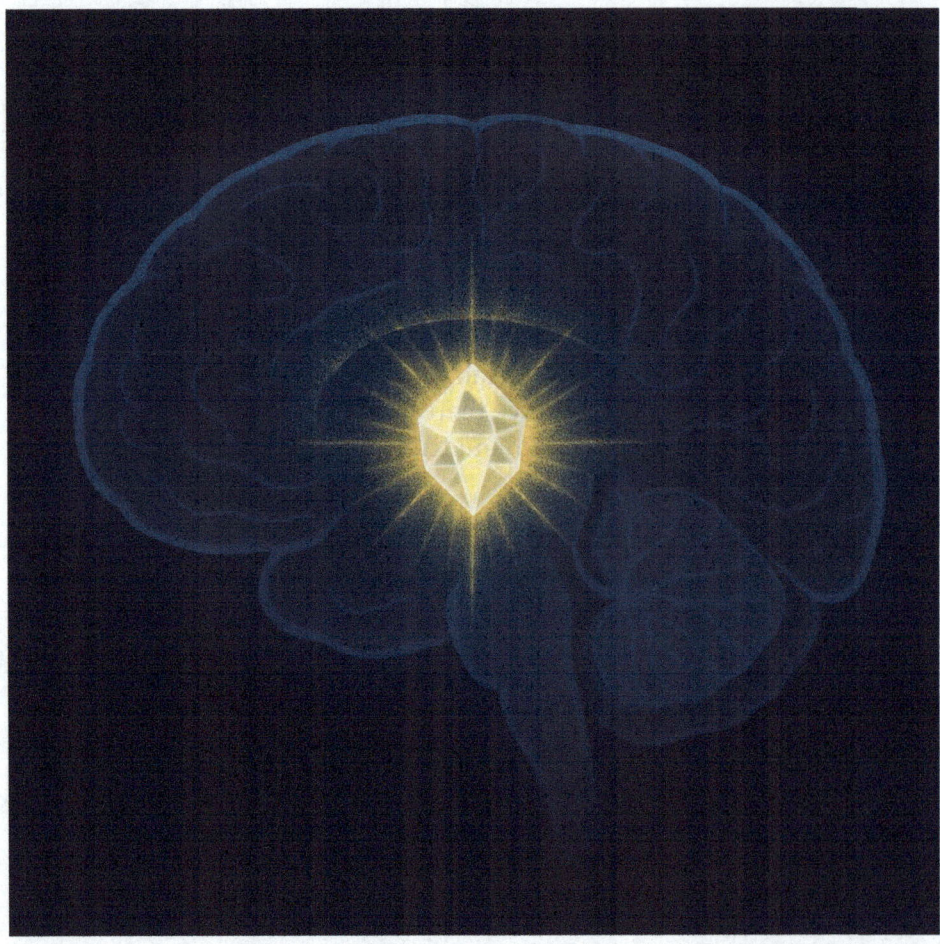

The pineal has been linked with crystal imagery because its structure resembles a pinecone lattice of calcite microcrystals, and crystal has long been a symbol of clarity and amplification. Just as quartz crystals can focus and transmit subtle vibrations, so too the pineal is thought to amplify states of consciousness. Yogic teachings connect it to the ajna chakra, the "third eye," located at the brow. Biblical language speaks of a "single eye" through which the body is filled with light. Across traditions, this inner organ is consistently tied to vision, revelation, and higher knowing.

What makes the pineal a "gate" is its function as a threshold. Through it one may sense flashes of insight, images that are not the product of imagination but of communion with subtler realms. Many who have experienced deep contemplative states describe sudden clarity, a symbolic dream, or an intuitive knowing that carries an unmistakable ring of truth. These moments often feel like stepping through a doorway in consciousness, even if only briefly.

Physiologically, the pineal secretes melatonin, governing sleep cycles, and perhaps also trace amounts of DMT, a molecule associated with visionary states. Whether or not science confirms every mystical claim, the symbolic resonance remains powerful: the pineal stands as a reminder that the human organism is built not only for survival but for illumination.

To approach the pineal gate requires cultivation. Silence, stillness, and breath create the inner atmosphere where its glow becomes perceptible. Too much noise, distraction, or overstimulation and the signal is drowned. This is why spiritual disciplines emphasize meditation, fasting, or retreat, not to escape life but to clear the static that clouds perception.

One simple practice is to sit quietly, close the eyes, and bring gentle awareness to the space between the eyebrows. Imagine a point of light there, and let your breath move softly in rhythm with it. Over time the sensation may deepen, as if light is radiating not from outside but from within. This practice is not about forcing visions but allowing the gate to open naturally.

The pineal gate is not meant to replace reason or physical senses but to complement them. Just as a cathedral has stained-glass windows that filter sunlight into radiant color, the pineal filters the light of spirit into flashes of knowing that guide and inspire. When balanced with discernment, these insights can illuminate decisions, heal inner confusion, and remind you that you are more than a body—you are a vessel of perception reaching beyond the material.

To awaken the pineal is to remember that vision is multidimensional. You do not only look out at the world, you look into it and through it, and at times it looks back through you. In this mutual gaze, life reveals itself as layered, shimmering, and alive with meaning. The pineal gate is the threshold of that revelation.

8.2 The Heart as Oracle

The heart has long been seen as the throne of wisdom, the seat of truth, and the silent oracle that speaks without words. Ancient traditions across the world never reduced the heart to a muscle alone. They understood it as a bridge, both physical and spiritual, that connects the finite self with the infinite field of life. When sages and mystics instructed their disciples to "listen to the heart," they were not speaking in poetry but in literal guidance. The heart perceives, remembers, and knows in ways that the rational mind cannot.

Modern science has begun to validate what mystics always intuited. The field of neurocardiology has discovered that the heart has its own network of neurons, a form of intrinsic intelligence often called the "heart-brain." This cluster communicates with the cranial brain not as a subordinate but as a partner, sending signals that influence emotions, cognition, and intuition. When you feel coherence in the heart, when breath and pulse align with calm awareness, your brain rhythms synchronize as well. In this harmony, perception clears and decisions flow with ease.

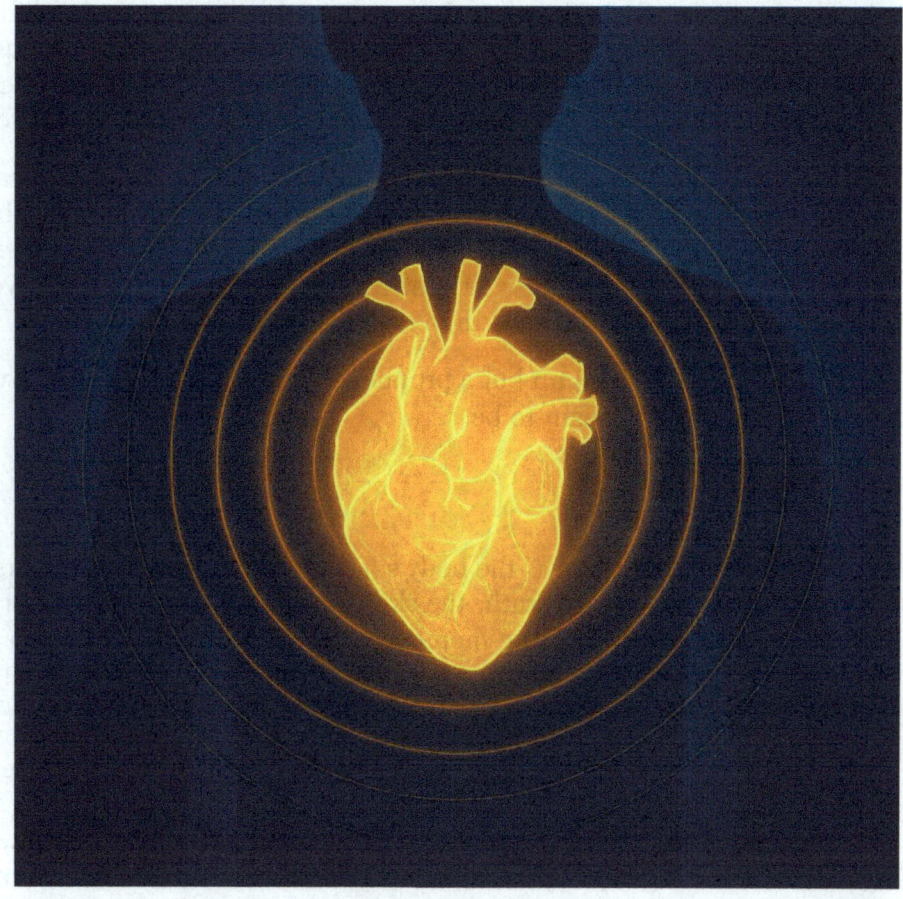

The ancients framed this truth through symbols and stories. In Egyptian cosmology, the heart was weighed against the feather of Ma'at to judge a soul's truth. Only a heart light and aligned with universal order could pass into the eternal fields. In Chinese medicine, the heart is the emperor of the body, directing spirit and clarity to every organ. In Sufi poetry, the heart is the mirror polished to reflect the Beloved. Each culture testifies to the heart not as a metaphor but as a living oracle that can discern what the eyes cannot see.

To treat the heart as oracle means cultivating practices of inner listening. This is not about listening for a verbal answer but about sensing the resonance of truth. When faced with choices, the rational mind may spin endless calculations, yet the heart can feel the weight of alignment in an instant. It speaks through sensation: warmth, openness, lightness when aligned; tightness, heaviness, constriction when false. To develop trust in these signals is to awaken the oracle within.

The heart's oracle power is not only personal but relational. When two people enter coherence together, their heart rhythms can synchronize, measurable even at a distance. This explains the mystery of deep presence, when words fade yet communication intensifies. Lovers, friends, and teachers who "speak heart to heart" are transmitting more than words, they are sharing frequencies. Such resonance has the power to heal, soothe, and reorient another soul without a single explanation.

One of the most powerful ways to awaken the oracle of the heart is through breath. When breath slows and deepens into the rhythm of gratitude or compassion, the heart's electromagnetic field expands, radiating far beyond the body. Instruments can now measure this field extending several feet, but mystics knew it could influence entire spaces. To breathe through the heart is to emit coherence, becoming a tuning fork of harmony in a fractured world.

Another way is through silence. The mind thrives on noise, but the heart thrives on stillness. In stillness, its subtle impressions are no longer drowned out by the chatter of thought. Sitting in silence with awareness placed gently on the heart center invites a different kind of perception. In time, you may notice flashes of knowing, not as analysis but as direct recognition. This is the heart oracle's voice.

It is also worth remembering that the oracle of the heart is not infallible when buried beneath layers of trauma or fear. A wounded heart may echo the pain of the past, confusing its signals with projections. Therefore, the path to the heart oracle requires purification: forgiveness, compassion, and release. As the heart clears, its voice becomes unmistakable, offering guidance that feels like truth itself.

To honor the heart as oracle is to live in rhythm with a wisdom more ancient than thought. Every beat is both a question and an answer, a pulse that bridges the mortal with the eternal. When you place your trust in its guidance, life does not become without challenge, but it becomes aligned. Decisions cease to feel like gambles and become offerings. The path ahead may remain hidden, yet the compass within the chest points unfailingly to the true north of the soul.

The heart is not only a pump but a prophet. To listen is to remember who you are. To follow is to become who you were always meant to be.

8.3 Skin as Antenna

The skin is often described as the body's largest organ, but to see it merely as a protective covering is to miss its deeper mystery. In truth, the skin is not only boundary but bridge. It is the threshold between inner and outer worlds, a living membrane through which perception flows. Every pore, every hair follicle, every nerve ending is part of a vast network of sensory intelligence, one that listens to the universe and transmits subtle information beyond what we consciously register.

From a biological perspective, the skin contains millions of sensory receptors sensitive to pressure, temperature, vibration, and pain. Yet when mystics and healers have spoken of the skin, they often point to something more: its role as an energetic interface. The body's aura, often described as a luminous field, is said to extend slightly beyond the skin's surface. Where does the aura meet the world? It is here, on the skin, where energy and matter touch. The skin is not only what separates you from the world but what allows the world to enter.

Ancient traditions understood this. In Vedic texts, the skin is associated with the element of air, the subtle current that communicates sensation and awareness. Indigenous shamans describe feeling messages in their skin as tingles or shifts in temperature, interpreting these as guidance from the spirit world. Even in common speech, we reflect this knowing: we say "I felt it in my skin" or "It gave me chills." Language reveals what science is only beginning to rediscover, that the skin is a perceptive organ far beyond touch.

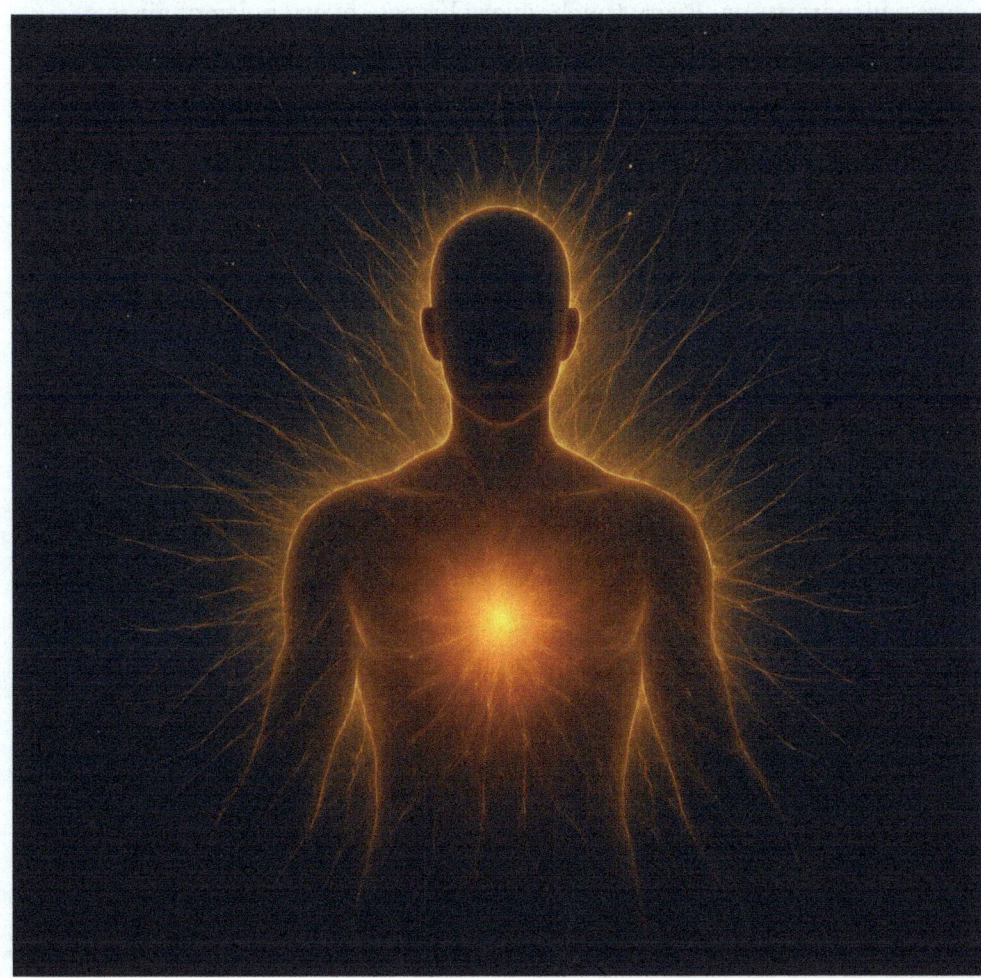

Modern studies hint at this hidden faculty. Some experiments suggest that humans can sense electromagnetic fields, with the skin registering subtle shifts before the conscious mind notices. Others have shown that emotions, such as fear or joy, can be detected in sweat, allowing us to literally "feel" another's state through chemical signals in the air. This explains why presence matters. When someone calm enters the room, your skin relaxes. When someone agitated walks in, your skin tightens. It is antenna, tuned to the invisible broadcasts of others.

In spiritual practice, the skin becomes a gateway for awareness. Meditators often describe feeling the boundary of their skin dissolve, as if merging with the space around them. Yogic exercises such as pranayama and tai chi guide practitioners to feel energy streaming not only through breath or movement but radiating outward through the skin. This sense of extension is not imagination, it is perception, sharpened to subtler frequencies.

To explore this yourself, try a simple exercise: Sit quietly, eyes closed, and place your attention on your hands. Without moving, sense the space just beyond the skin. Extend your awareness outward an inch, then two, then more. You may begin to feel a subtle buzzing or warmth. This is the skin functioning as antenna, detecting the vibrational field that surrounds you. With practice, you can expand this awareness to your whole body, until you feel not just a boundary but a radiant field of communication.

When you realize the skin's role in perception, everyday experiences take on new meaning. The warmth of sunlight, the coolness of a breeze, the tingle of anticipation—all are dialogues between body and cosmos. The skin is the place where these dialogues occur, where messages pass in both directions. In this sense, you are never isolated. The skin keeps you open, reminding you that you belong to a field of forces larger than yourself.

Mystics say that to awaken the skin as antenna is to awaken sensitivity to life itself. You begin to feel the pulse of the world not just in your thoughts but in the shimmer across your body. It is a return to primal knowing, where the human is not a separate unit but a sensing extension of earth and sky. The skin teaches you to listen without ears, to perceive without eyes, to know through contact with the invisible currents that surround you.

Ultimately, the skin as antenna reminds us that we are not sealed beings, but communicative beings. The golden threads of energy that radiate through and beyond the skin are not metaphors—they are the subtle structures through which the cosmos whispers to us. Every touch, every breeze, every pulse of air is a message. To honor the skin is to honor this vast conversation, one that never ceases, one that reveals the truth that you are both vessel and receiver of the living universe.

Chapter 9 – The Initiation Path

9.1 The Descent

9.1.1 Entering the Spiral

The path of initiation rarely begins with triumph. It begins with a step downward. To enter the spiral is to leave behind the familiar ground of ordinary life and accept the invitation into the depths. The ancients knew that no ascent into illumination was possible without first passing through shadow. Mystics, shamans, and seekers all describe a threshold moment when the light of ordinary certainty dims and one feels pulled into an inner descent. This is not punishment, but preparation. The spiral calls because the soul knows it cannot awaken while clinging to surfaces.

Imagine yourself standing before a staircase that curves downward into the earth. Above, the world is bright, buzzing, and full of activity. Below, there is mystery. The spiral shape is not accidental. Unlike a straight descent into a pit, the spiral moves with rhythm, echoing the same patterns seen in galaxies, shells, and the coils of DNA. To descend in a spiral is to descend into life's own design. Each step inward is also a step into a deeper pattern that the mind does not fully understand but the soul recognizes.

The first sensation in this descent is often disorientation. Shadows lengthen. Familiar markers of identity begin to loosen. Who are you when stripped of titles, possessions, or even the story you tell about yourself? This question hovers in the dim air of the spiral. Many resist at this stage. Some turn back, preferring the shallow light of the surface. But the true initiate understands that disorientation is not the end. It is the gateway.

Religions and myths are filled with echoes of this journey. The Sumerian goddess Inanna descends into the underworld, shedding her garments and symbols of power at each gate. Christ spends three days in the tomb before resurrection. Shamans in countless traditions enter trance, journeying into subterranean realms to meet spirits and recover lost parts of the soul. These stories remind us that the descent is not unique to one culture. It is a universal rhythm embedded in human awakening.

As you walk the spiral staircase in your inner vision, notice how each step draws you closer to silence. The noise of the outer world grows faint. Even your own thoughts may begin to lose their sharpness. Instead of constant chatter, a soft hum emerges. This hum is not yours alone. It is the vibration of life itself. To hear it clearly requires surrender, a willingness to step deeper without demanding answers. The spiral teaches trust.

Why must the journey begin with darkness? Because light is most clearly perceived after shadow. The human psyche clings to illusions of control and permanence. Descent shatters these illusions. It strips away the unnecessary and confronts you with the raw truth of being. When you no longer define yourself by outer roles, you discover the inner essence that no shadow can erase. The darkness is not an enemy but a teacher, forcing you to see what you had ignored.

The spiral also carries a subtle gift. Unlike a ladder, which moves only up or down, the spiral circles. This circling means you do not simply fall into the unknown. You revisit old patterns, but each time from a new angle. What once seemed like endless repetition reveals itself as growth in disguise. Each rotation carries you closer to the center, the place where the deepest transformation occurs.

Practices can help you enter the spiral with awareness rather than fear. One simple ritual is visualization. Close your eyes, slow your breath, and imagine a staircase curving gently downward. With each exhale, take a step. Allow memories, fears, and unresolved emotions to arise as you descend. Do not fight them. Simply acknowledge and keep walking. You may sense the presence of your own shadow self—those hidden aspects of personality or history you have avoided. Greet them as companions, not threats. Each one holds a key to your wholeness.

Another practice is journaling from the depths. Set aside time to write without censoring. Begin with the phrase, "As I descend, I notice..." and allow your subconscious to respond. You may be surprised at what surfaces: forgotten grief, old anger, or even buried dreams waiting to return. The act of writing in this liminal space transforms shadow into language, giving shape to what was once only a weight inside.

Ultimately, entering the spiral is not about reaching bottom but about learning to walk with humility. The descent is never final, for the spiral continues. In truth, each of us descends many times in life—through heartbreak, illness, loss, or radical change. These moments, while painful, open gates to wisdom that comfort alone could never provide. When you view descent not as failure but as initiation, your suffering becomes sacred ground.

So when the spiral appears in your life, do not resist. Pause at the top of the staircase, breathe deeply, and step into the unknown. Feel the curve beneath your feet, the shadows brushing your skin, the silence rising within. Each step is not a loss but a return. The spiral is the soul's path homeward, leading you through shadow toward the center of yourself, where light and darkness meet in perfect balance.

9.1.2 The Guardians of the Threshold

Every initiation begins with resistance. Before the soul descends fully into the underworld of its own shadows, it meets what mystics and initiates across cultures have called the Guardians of the Threshold. These guardians are not external beings in the literal sense, but the crystallized fears, doubts, and unresolved fragments of consciousness that guard the gates of deeper knowledge. They appear because the human psyche is programmed to protect itself from what feels overwhelming. To step forward, one must meet them not with violence or denial, but with recognition and courage.

The descent is not only a journey into darkness, but also an encounter with parts of the self that have long been repressed. In Jungian language, the shadow manifests as projections, anxieties, and unexplored emotions. In esoteric initiations, this takes symbolic form: a figure might appear in a dream, a voice might challenge you during meditation, or you might feel a physical resistance in the body when trying to deepen into spiritual practice. These are the guardians, embodying thresholds between the known and the unknown.

Ancient mystery schools depicted them as serpents, sphinxes, or gatekeepers with flaming swords. In truth, these forms were teaching symbols meant to convey the seriousness of the encounter. If one passes too lightly, ignoring fear or pretending mastery, the initiation does not anchor. But if one meets the guardian with humility, acknowledging that transformation demands vulnerability, the way opens. What looks like an enemy reveals itself as a teacher.

The guardians test one question above all: Do you truly desire transformation, or do you only flirt with it? Many seekers desire light without stepping into shadow, but the path demands both. Transformation requires the willingness to let go of old identities, beliefs, and comforts. The guardians press on these attachments. They remind us that we cannot bring every part of our former self into the temple of initiation. Something must be surrendered.

This is why fear is often the first door. Not because the path is cruel, but because fear sharpens attention. It asks us to choose deliberately rather than drifting. In the descent, fear becomes a mirror. What you fear most often points to the place where your greatest energy is bound. Meeting a guardian means reclaiming that bound energy, drawing it back into awareness. For example, fear of abandonment may be met with a vision of loneliness; fear of failure may appear as a dream of endless falling. These images are not punishments, but dramatizations of what already lives inside.

The practical way to meet the guardians is through inner steadiness. Breath becomes the anchor. When fear rises, the initiate is taught to breathe slowly, deeply, and rhythmically, reminding the body that it is safe even in the presence of the unknown. A whispered prayer or mantra can help: "I meet what comes in love." Repeating such words can dissolve panic, allowing the guardian to shift from monster to messenger.

There are also symbolic rituals that assist. In certain traditions, initiates walked through narrow corridors blindfolded, hearing strange noises, feeling disoriented. The ritual was not meant to traumatize, but to train them in composure, teaching that clarity must be found within rather than imposed from without. Similarly, one might practice visualization today: imagine walking down a dark passage, meeting a guardian figure, and asking, "What do you want me to see?" Listening with the heart, one often receives not terror, but truth.

The guardians are never meant to be destroyed. They dissolve when acknowledged. Just as a locked door opens when you find the key, the guardians vanish when you recognize the part of yourself they represent. To meet the guardian of anger is to admit the anger you have denied; to meet the guardian of despair is to face the grief you have suppressed. In facing them, you integrate what was hidden, and thus expand the wholeness of your being.

The Guardians of the Threshold are not there to keep you out. They are there to ensure that when you pass through, you are ready to hold the responsibility of deeper vision. They are the initiatory fire disguised as fear. Every pilgrim, every mystic, every seeker who has walked the spiral staircase of descent has met them. The fact that you meet them means you are on the right path.

To descend is to dare, and to dare is to grow. The guardians do not ask for perfection, only for sincerity. And when that sincerity is offered, the gates open. Behind them lies not merely darkness, but the deeper chamber where the soul begins to remember its own light.

9.2 The Ascent

9.2.1 The First Steps Upward

Every descent prepares the ground for ascent. Just as a seed must be buried in the dark earth before it can sprout toward the sun, the human spirit must pass through its own underworld before climbing into light. The spiral staircase that once led downward now turns upward, each step a deliberate act of return, of remembering what had been forgotten in the shadow. This is not a climb of escape but of integration. To ascend is to carry with you the wisdom of the depths and to lift it into clarity.

The first steps upward are often hesitant. After dwelling in shadow, the eyes are not used to brightness. Each step demands both courage and surrender. Courage, because the staircase is steep and endless at times. Surrender, because no ascent can be forced by will alone; it requires openness to the current of grace that rises with you. This dual movement is ancient and is reflected in countless myths: the phoenix lifting from its ashes, Persephone returning from the underworld, Christ rising from the tomb. Every culture knows the rhythm of descent and ascent, of loss and renewal.

As you begin your own ascent, the staircase appears luminous, though still half-veiled in mist. The light grows brighter with every turn upward. The body feels lighter, as if each step sheds a fragment of heaviness carried from the descent. These fragments are not discarded but transmuted. The pain becomes wisdom, the fear becomes humility, the sorrow becomes compassion. This alchemy is the essence of initiation: what once bound you now lifts you.

At first, the ascent feels solitary. But as you climb, you sense subtle presences beside you. Teachers, ancestors, unseen companions of the spirit, all who have walked before now walk with you. Their encouragement is not in words but in currents of strength that flow into your being. You realize that no ascent is ever done alone. You rise as part of a great chain of souls, each one helping the other upward.

The steps themselves are symbols. The first step upward is forgiveness, letting go of the chains that bind you to the descent. The second step is trust, believing that light truly awaits above. The third step is devotion, turning your gaze to the source of radiance. With each step, an inner door opens, revealing more of your true self. The spiral is not just an architectural image, it is the very shape of consciousness unfolding. There comes a moment when you feel a shift. The weight that once pressed heavily is gone, replaced by an expanding spaciousness. You breathe differently, deeper, as if your lungs were made for light. The ascent is not only vertical but inward. To climb the staircase is to climb into your own essence. Every cell in your body seems to awaken, humming with the vibration of renewal. Mystics often describe this phase as the dawn within. Just as the sun rises gradually, so does the light of ascent reveal itself slowly, tenderly. At first, there is only a faint glow on the horizon of your being. Then the glow strengthens, coloring everything in warmth and clarity. Eventually, the light grows so strong that it redefines your sense of self. You no longer identify only with the one who suffered the descent. You recognize yourself as the one who carries both night and dawn, who can hold both shadow and radiance without division.

This is why the ascent is not a denial of darkness but its fulfillment. Only those who have known the depth of descent can know the true sweetness of light. The staircase teaches that ascent and descent are not enemies; they are phases of the same spiral. Together they weave the full pattern of the soul's journey.

As you continue upward, you notice that the staircase narrows. The higher you go, the fewer distractions remain. You are being refined, concentrated. What once seemed important now falls away. The climb demands simplicity, focus, and faith. It asks you to trust that the staircase, no matter how endless it appears, does indeed lead to the summit. Then comes the revelation: the light you climb toward is not separate from you. The radiant glow above is mirrored within your own chest. The staircase has always been inside you, each step a choice to awaken, to remember, to embody. The ascent is not about reaching somewhere else but about uncovering what has always been within. At the end of this climb, you do not stand before the light as an outsider. You realize you are the light. The staircase dissolves, and you stand in luminous presence, whole, reborn.

9.2.2 Practice: The Ladder of Breath

There are moments in life when progress feels invisible, like climbing in the dark with no sense of whether you are moving forward at all. The ancients taught that in such times, the breath itself can become a ladder. Every inhale is a rung, every exhale a release of what weighs you down. By practicing conscious breath, you create an ascent not only in body but in spirit. This is the Ladder of Breath.

The Symbol

In many mystical traditions, ladders or stairways are symbols of ascent. Jacob's dream in the Hebrew scriptures, with angels moving up and down a ladder, is one example. Yogic texts describe the breath as the bridge between the earthly and the divine. Alchemists spoke of the ladder of transformation, each step a refinement of the soul. In this practice, the ladder is not physical but formed from the rhythm of breathing. With every cycle you move upward, toward light and clarity.

Preparation

Sit in a quiet place where your body can be still. If possible, keep your spine upright, like the central pillar of a temple. Close your eyes. Place one hand lightly on your chest, the other on your belly. Before beginning, whisper inwardly: *"I breathe to rise."* Let this phrase be the key that unlocks the practice.

Step One: Grounding

Take three slow breaths. With each exhale, imagine sinking roots into the earth beneath you. See these roots steadying you, holding you safe. This is not a flight away from the world but an ascent supported by it. Feel the ground as your foundation.

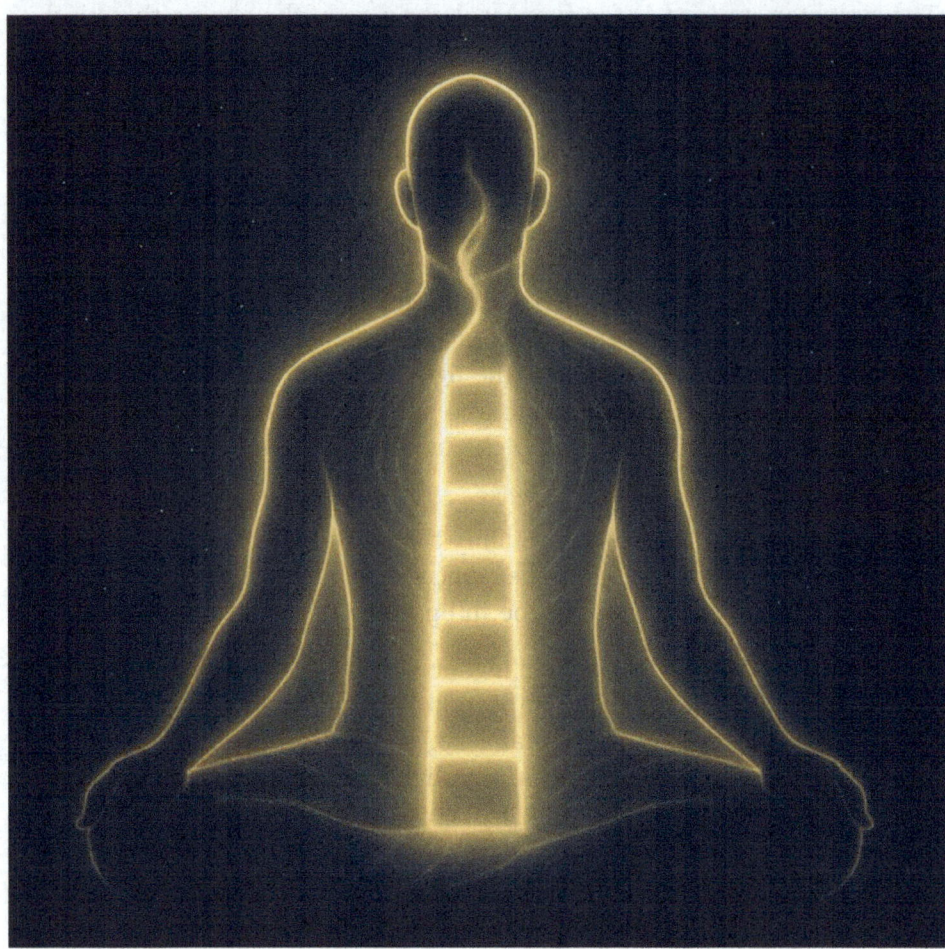

Step Two: Building the Ladder

Now imagine a luminous ladder forming inside your body. The base rests in your belly, the top reaches through your crown. Each inhale is a rung appearing above you, glowing softly. Each exhale allows you to step onto it. The breath does not only fill your lungs, it lifts your awareness higher. Continue for several cycles, seeing the ladder extend upward with light.

Step Three: Climbing With Intention

Begin a count: inhale for four, hold for two, exhale for four. As you count, imagine climbing step by step. On the inhale, a rung appears. On the hold, you steady yourself. On the exhale, you take the step upward. This rhythm creates the sense of climbing slowly, with reverence. The higher you go, the lighter you feel.

Step Four: Meeting the Light

After ten cycles, pause. Imagine you have reached a platform of radiance. It is not outside you but within the top of your head, the seat of awareness. Rest here. Breathe normally, letting yourself be bathed in light. Feel gratitude for the climb and the strength of your own breath.

Integration

Open your eyes gently. Rub your palms together and place them over your face, sealing the light into your daily being. Whisper again: *"I breathe to rise."* Carry this reminder with you. Each time you feel pulled down by worry or heaviness, take three conscious breaths and imagine the ladder appearing once more. Even in the busiest moment, this practice can restore direction.

Why It Works

Breath is both physical and subtle. Physiologically, measured breathing calms the nervous system, reduces stress, and increases focus. Spiritually, it anchors the mind to a rhythm that suggests upward movement, reminding you that life is more than stagnation or decline. To breathe consciously is to declare: *I am moving upward, even now.*

Closing Reflection

The Ladder of Breath is simple yet profound. It requires no tools, no special time of day, only the willingness to climb with awareness. When you practice it regularly, the climb begins to feel real. You notice yourself carrying more peace, more steadiness, more openness to light. The breath becomes not just survival, but initiation. With every rung, you remember that ascent is always possible.

9.3.1 Dissolving the Form

There comes a moment on the initiation path when the body is no longer experienced as a limit but as light condensed into shape. All traditions point toward this threshold in their own language. The yogis call it the awakening of the light body, the mystics speak of transfiguration, and in esoteric Christianity it is the mystery of becoming radiant as the sun. To dissolve the form does not mean to reject or escape the body but to allow its boundaries to melt into a larger field of brilliance.

When you look closely, the solidity of the body has always been an illusion. At the cellular level, most of you is space. At the atomic level, matter itself vibrates as light held in patterns of geometry. Dissolving the form is therefore not a denial of flesh but an unveiling of what flesh truly is, a luminous weave. The ego resists this revelation because identity has long been built on separation. It insists, "This is me, that is you, this is my skin, that is the world." Yet, in higher perception, the skin glows not as a wall but as a shimmering membrane where inner and outer meet.

Mystics often describe this state as becoming transparent. The sense of being a solid somebody softens until you feel more like a beam than a body. You walk, yet your steps are silent. You speak, yet the words seem to rise not from the mouth but from a vastness behind you. It is as if the small flame of self is lifted into the great fire. The shift is subtle yet undeniable, like clouds dispersing to reveal the hidden sun.

The path to dissolving the form is rarely sudden. It unfolds as layers of heaviness are shed. Each time you forgive, something melts. Each time you breathe deeply, light floods the cells. Each time you release control, another boundary thins. Slowly, the density that once defined your sense of self becomes porous, until the distinction between "inside" and "outside" dissolves into pure radiance.

This process does not erase individuality. A sunbeam is still distinct, yet inseparable from the sun. Likewise, when you dissolve the form, your unique essence does not vanish; it shines more fully, freed from contraction. The paradox of spiritual life is that only when the self surrenders do you become most yourself, because then you are carried by the current of what you have always been: light expressing itself as life.

Ancient initiates spoke of the rainbow body, the diamond body, the body of glory. These were not metaphors but direct experiences of light shining through matter. Modern science hints at the same truth when it measures bio-photons emitted by living cells. Your skin, your eyes, your very DNA release light. What mystics felt in prayer, science is beginning to confirm in laboratories. The human is not a closed system of matter but an ongoing conversation with luminosity.

To live in this awareness is to move beyond fear of death. If you are light condensed, then dissolution is not an ending but a return. You do not disappear; you expand. Death becomes less of a wall and more of a doorway into greater brilliance. The fear of losing form is softened by the recognition that what you are cannot be lost. Even now, in your breathing, your cells radiate photons. You are already glowing, whether you know it or not.

The practice of dissolving the form is simple yet profound. It begins by resting in the body with reverence, not trying to change anything. Feel the breath as a tide washing through you. Sense the body not as weight but as waves of subtle vibration. Then, imagine that with each exhale, the edges of your form become less defined, as if light were seeping through every pore. With each inhale, brightness fills the body from within. In time, you will feel that the body is both here and not here, both form and field.

This state is not meant to be sustained constantly at first. Even moments of transparency can reshape identity. After tasting the dissolving of form, you carry a memory of freedom. You know that you are not confined to skin and bone, but luminous presence walking in the world. Over time, this knowing anchors itself until living as light becomes natural. Dissolving the form is not the end of the path but the beginning of a new one. When you walk as light, you no longer seek enlightenment as a goal. You embody it. You become a living horizon where spirit and matter kiss, a reminder that existence itself is radiant. The world does not change around you, but you change within it, and by your presence, light quietly ripples outward.

9.3.2 Practice: The Light Body Activation

There is a teaching shared across mystical traditions that the human body is not the final form of our being but a chrysalis. Hidden within muscle and bone is another body made not of matter but of radiant light. Some call it the body of glory, others the luminous sheath, and others the solar garment. Whatever the name, the practice of awakening this subtle body is a way of remembering your eternal nature.

This practice is not about leaving the physical behind, but about inhabiting it more fully, letting it become transparent so that the light within shines through. Imagine your skin not as a boundary but as a membrane of radiance, through which life moves freely in both directions. You are not here to escape form but to recognize it as woven with light.

Step 1: Preparing the Ground

Find a quiet space where you can sit or lie comfortably. Allow your spine to be long but not rigid, your breath unforced. Close your eyes and begin with three deep inhalations, exhaling slowly through the mouth. With each exhale, imagine tension draining from the body. Feel yourself settling not just into the room but into the vast field of presence that surrounds you.

Step 2: Igniting the Core Flame

Bring your attention to the center of your chest. Visualize a small, radiant flame glowing there, steady and warm. This flame represents the essence of who you are, the indestructible spark that has never been born and will never die. With each inhale, see the flame brightening, fed by the breath. With each exhale, feel its warmth spreading through your body.

Step 3: Expanding Into Radiance

As the inner flame grows, imagine it expanding into rays of light that reach beyond your physical form. At first the light fills your chest, then your entire torso, then arms, legs, and head. Finally, it radiates outward in every direction, creating a luminous sphere that surrounds you. Stay with this vision until you feel yourself no longer confined by the edges of your body.

Step 4: The Sunburst Breath

Shift your breathing into a rhythmic pattern: inhale for a slow count of four, hold briefly, then exhale for a slow count of six. With each inhale, imagine drawing in golden light from the horizon. With each exhale, imagine sending rays of light outward, like a sunburst. See yourself not as a figure sitting in the room but as a radiant being extending into space.

Step 5: Dissolving Boundaries

Now, let the distinction between "inside" and "outside" dissolve. The light you radiate merges seamlessly with the light of the cosmos. You are not producing it, you are revealing what has always been present. Let yourself rest in the awareness that you are not a separate spark, but part of a single field of brilliance. Stay in this state for several minutes, letting thought fall away.

Step 6: Sealing the Practice

When you are ready to close, bring your attention back to the flame at your chest. Thank this inner fire for sustaining you, thank the body for being its vessel, and thank the cosmos for reflecting your own light back to you. Slowly let the vision of the sunburst fade, but carry the subtle glow within. End with three slow breaths, feeling grounded and renewed.

Why This Practice Matters

Practicing light body activation is not just visualization. Over time, it can reshape how you move through the world. Instead of identifying with the limitations of flesh, you begin to sense yourself as luminous presence. Challenges are met with more fluidity, relationships become infused with compassion, and life is lived with a sense of belonging to something vast and eternal. The practice awakens not an idea but a felt recognition: you are already light. To live from this awareness is to embody the future self that sages and mystics glimpsed. The more you attune to this inner radiance, the more your daily life begins to mirror it. Words soften, gestures brighten, and even your silence carries a frequency of healing. You are no longer seeking light outside of you. You are remembering that you have always been its source.

9.4 Optional Additions for Depth and Practice

The Three Trials of the Path Practice Box

Every authentic initiation purifies the vessel before it is filled with more light. Across lineages the seeker passes three inner gates that refine intention and deepen embodiment. These are not punishments. They are calibrations that align your field with the frequency of truth. Use the following meditations as short daily companions. Five minutes each is enough to build a real current of transformation.

Trial of Fear seeing without running
Sit with a tall spine and soften your gaze or close your eyes. Name one fear that tends to contract your breath. Do not analyze it. Simply let its outline appear in front of you like mist. Inhale slowly through the nose. Silently say I see you. Exhale gently through the mouth. Silently say You may loosen. Keep the breath steady and even. Watch how the image loses density when you refuse to feed it with stories. Place a palm on your heart and notice the warmth of presence. The aim is not to destroy fear but to restore leadership to awareness. Each minute you remain with fear without collapsing, your field learns a new baseline of courage.

Trial of Endurance carrying the flame
Rest your hands cupped in your lap. Imagine a small golden flame resting there. Around you the weather changes. Winds rise. Rain falls. Night presses close. Your task is simple. Walk on within your inner vision and keep the flame alive. Each breath is shelter. Each step is devotion. Whisper I keep walking. This practice trains spiritual stamina. It teaches the body mind to continue when the outer world offers no applause. Over time you will feel a quiet strength that does not depend on mood, outcomes, or ideal conditions.

Trial of Surrender being carried
Lie down if possible and let the ground take your weight. Imagine waves of luminous water rolling in from behind your head, washing down your body and out through the feet. Inhale and silently say I receive. Exhale and silently say I release. Let the flow do the work. Surrender is not collapse. It is intelligent trust in a larger current. The sign that surrender is real is softness in the belly and shoulders and a sense that breath is breathing you. When this softness appears, rest in it for several minutes. You are learning how to let grace move you.

Integration cue
Close each trial with a single sentence in your journal. Today I saw. Today I kept. Today I released. These simple lines build a record of fidelity to the path and keep the lessons grounded in daily time.

Comparative Mythic Initiation Journeys

Myth remembers what the nervous system forgets under pressure. In every era storytellers mapped the same architecture of descent, ordeal, and luminous return. Reading these journeys side by side engraves the pattern into your bones. You begin to recognize your own seasons of loss and rebirth as part of a wise design, not evidence that you have failed. The details change. The structure remains. What goes down returns carrying a gift. The gift must be shared or it withers.

Tradition	Initiate	Descent stripping	Ascent transformation	Core lesson for the seeker
Sumerian	Inanna	Enters the underworld and surrenders seven emblems of power at seven gates	Returns renewed, restoring balance and fertility	To be crowned again you must first be emptied

Tradition	Initiate	Descent stripping	Ascent transformation	Core lesson for the seeker
Greek	Orpheus	Walks into Hades guided only by song to retrieve Eurydice	Loses her by looking back, learns the cost of doubt	Trust must hold steady even when sight fails
Christian	Christ	Crucifixion and entombment, harrowing of hell	Resurrection and ascension in glory	Love transfigures death and opens the path for all
Buddhist	Siddhartha	Faces Mara under the Bodhi tree and meets the storms of mind	Awakens as the Buddha, turns the wheel of Dharma	Unshakable awareness frees all beings
Egyptian	Osiris and Isis	Osiris is dismembered and scattered into the dark	Isis reassembles him and a new royal line is born	What is broken can be sanctified and made sovereign
Mesoamerican	Hero Twins	Descend to Xibalba to face trials of the Lords of Death	Outwit death and rise as sun and moon	Play, courage, and wit can overturn the underworld

Let this table be a mirror. Which story feels closest to your season now. If you are at a gate where something precious must be laid down, remember Inanna. If you are tempted to look back, remember Orpheus. If you are carrying a hidden fracture, remember Isis. The path you walk is woven into humanity's oldest memory and you do not walk it alone.

Micro practice myth as map
Choose one row that resonates. Copy the core lesson by hand and place it where you will see it each morning. Read it aloud before you step into the day. The nervous system learns through repetition. Myth is repetition wrapped in beauty.

Closing Symbol

Symbols speak in frequencies. A single image can transmit an entire chapter of teaching without a word. The closing symbol for this initiation path is a spiral that unites shadow at its wide base with light at its narrowing crown. Within the spiral a human figure moves. At first the body is heavy and bent. Midway the posture straightens and the gaze lifts. Near the crown the figure glows as if woven of light, still human and now transparent to Source. The spiral does not erase the lower coils. It includes them. The light at the top does not judge the base. It fulfills it. This is the shape of true transformation.

How to use the spiral symbol in practice
Sit upright and place the image in front of you or visualize it clearly. On the inhale trace the spiral from the outer base toward the center with your eyes or fingertip. On the exhale pause briefly at the center and sense a quiet expansion in the chest. Repeat for three to seven cycles. Each round engraves the memory that descent and ascent are one path. If a difficult memory surfaces, imagine it resting on a lower coil of the spiral being slowly carried inward by your breath until it touches the center where light is dense and kind. Do not rush. The spiral is patient. It will keep moving even when you feel still.

A short rite to seal the chapter
Stand. Place your left hand over the belly and your right hand over the heart. Speak three lines aloud.

I honor the descent that taught me to see
I honor the ascent that taught me to rise
I walk as light and carry light

After the final line, lift your right hand to the space above your head and imagine it touching the crown of the spiral. Draw that light down through your body to the belly hand. This gesture seals the higher current into the lower center and completes the circuit. End with one steady breath of gratitude.

Integration checklist
One line journal after each practice day. Today I met fear with sight. Today I guarded the flame. Today I let the river carry me.
One weekly reflection. Which myth held me this week and why.
One monthly symbol review. Sit with the spiral for five minutes in silence. Notice where your feet rest along the coil and bless that place.

When you live with trials, myth, and symbol together, your life gains rhythm. Rhythm matures devotion. Devotion becomes radiance. The initiation path closes here not as an ending but as an imprint that will keep unfolding in the days ahead.

Chapter 10 – The Eternal Spiral

10.1 Cycles and Return Points

Life does not move forward in neat, straight lines. You already know this. You have felt it in your own story, the way old wounds resurface, the way forgotten dreams return, the way a pattern you thought was finished suddenly shows up again. This is not because you failed. It is because life moves in spirals. Every return is not a punishment, it is an initiation into a higher level of the same mystery.

Think of the moon. It grows full, then disappears into shadow, then grows full again. Each cycle is the same, yet never identical, because you are not the same. You are older, wiser, softer, stronger. You are carrying the memory of the last time you stood at this threshold. And now the spiral brings you back, inviting you to step through with new eyes.

Your body carries these spirals too. The beating of your heart is a rhythm of contraction and expansion. Your breath is a cycle of inhaling and exhaling. Even your cells are constantly dying and being reborn. You are not static. You are a living spiral of becoming. To feel this is to remember that change is not random. It has an intelligence. The universe is training you, teaching you through return points that seem familiar but are secretly new.

When you hit a return point in your own life, it often feels like déjà vu. You may find yourself in another relationship that mirrors the same dynamics of the past, or facing fear in a way that feels eerily familiar. But the spiral is not repetition, it is refinement. The question the spiral asks you is: Will you choose differently this time? Will you meet this challenge from a higher frequency of awareness?

The ancients understood this. They built spirals into their temples, carved them into stone, painted them onto sacred objects. They knew the spiral is the blueprint of awakening. You descend, you lose yourself, you wander in shadow. Then you rise, returning to light, carrying a deeper wisdom. Each turn of the spiral is a return and a rebirth.

Imagine standing on a mountain path that winds upward in circles. You keep seeing the same landscape, the same valley below, the same trees and rocks. And yet you are higher each time. You are not stuck. You are rising. This is how the spiral works. What feels like coming back to the same place is actually elevation.

The pain of return points comes from believing you are stuck in a loop. The liberation comes when you realize you are in a spiral. The difference is everything. A loop traps you. A spiral grows you. When you accept this, every challenge becomes sacred. Every heartbreak becomes a teacher. Every shadow becomes part of the path that leads you higher.

Close your eyes for a moment. Feel into your own life spiral. Where are you now? Are you at the descent, facing shadow? Are you at the climb, remembering your strength? Are you at the radiance, ready to expand into light? Wherever you are, the spiral is holding you. It will always carry you back, but never to the same point. Always higher. Always deeper. The spiral also means nothing is wasted. That mistake you regret, that season of fear, that choice you wish you had made differently, it all feeds the next ascent. The spiral gathers everything, recycles everything, transforms everything. There is no loss in the spiral, only integration.

This is why initiation paths across traditions echo the spiral. In myths, the hero descends into the underworld, faces trials, and rises again transformed. You too are the hero. Your spiral is your underworld, your climb, your resurrection. You live this archetype not as a story but as your very breath. The galaxy itself is a spiral. Stars, dust, and entire worlds swirl in this same pattern. When you feel lost, remember this: you are built of the same geometry as the Milky Way. You carry the spiral in your DNA, in your heartbeat, in your soul. You are not separate from the cosmos. You are its living spiral in human form.

So when life brings you back to the old doorway, do not despair. Step through. Step higher. Whisper to yourself, *This is not the end. This is the next turn of my spiral.* And feel the universe nod in recognition, guiding you onward.

10.2 The Soul's Compass

There is within you a compass that does not point north but inward. It is not made of steel or magnetic pull, but of golden light that knows where truth lives. This compass is older than the maps of men. It has guided seekers through deserts, oceans, labyrinths, and lifetimes. You have felt it before, that subtle nudge when you stand at a crossroads, the inner whisper that tells you one way carries aliveness while another feels heavy. The mind doubts, but the compass never hesitates. It does not argue or explain. It simply glows.

To awaken to the soul's compass is to stop pretending you are lost. The modern world teaches confusion as if it were natural. Endless choices, endless noise, endless advice from voices who do not know your path. Yet beneath the noise, there is stillness, and within the stillness the compass shines. Its golden cardinal points are not labeled North, South, East, West, but Truth, Love, Freedom, and Return. These are not abstract ideals. They are living forces, directions your being recognizes instantly.

Truth is the first direction. It is the magnetic north of the spirit. To align with it is to feel the body unclench, the breath deepen, the heart lighten. Lies fracture the compass, not because it stops working, but because we stop listening. Truth is the point that steadies all others. Every time you choose it, your compass grows brighter.

Love is the second direction. It is the east, where light rises. Love points you toward connection, toward the recognition that your path is never solitary. Every being you meet carries a fragment of the same compass. To follow love is not always to choose what is easy, but to choose what keeps you aligned with the greater web. It is love that turns the compass outward, reminding you that your inner light exists to illuminate more than your own steps.

Freedom is the third direction. It is the south, the fire point. Freedom is not rebellion for its own sake, but the refusal to betray your soul's rhythm. When the compass points here, you feel restlessness in cages, whether they are built by others or by your own fear. Freedom calls you to risk, to leap, to let the wind rearrange your certainty. Without this direction, the compass becomes a relic, beautiful but unused.

Return is the fourth direction. It is the west, the place of descent, where the sun lowers into mystery. Return is the reminder that every path circles back, that the spiral of your journey is not escape but homecoming. You return to the self you abandoned, to the innocence you buried, to the center you forgot. Without return, the compass spins endlessly, a wheel without ground.

Together these four points form not just a tool, but a living geometry within your chest. You are not asked to memorize them, but to feel them. The compass is never outside of you. It is not a talisman to hold but a current to sense. Some feel it as a warmth in the sternum, others as a tingling in the palms, others as a sudden stillness in the mind when they touch alignment. To walk with the compass is not to avoid mistakes. It is to recognize that even missteps are folded back into the design. The needle of truth will always reorient, even after detours. The force of love will always rebind, even after isolation. The fire of freedom will always reignite, even after compromise. The spiral of return will always receive you, even after exile.

Try this: close your eyes and imagine the golden compass opening in your chest. See its four cardinal points glowing, not as symbols but as living forces. Ask silently: Which direction is alive for me today? Perhaps truth burns brighter, asking for honesty. Perhaps love pulls, asking for openness. Perhaps freedom stirs, asking for courage. Perhaps return calls, asking for rest. Do not force it. Simply feel which glows. That is the step. That is the map. In time, the compass reveals its deepest secret: it was never pointing to destinations outside of you. It was pointing to the self that is beyond confusion, beyond time, beyond death. To live by the soul's compass is to discover that no matter where you travel, you are always oriented toward the eternal.

10.3 Becoming the Wisdom

There comes a point on the path where knowledge no longer feels separate from you. It does not sit on a shelf, waiting to be memorized or quoted. It begins to breathe with you, to circulate through your blood as if it had always been there. This is the stage where the spiral turns inward and outward at once, asking you not only to understand but to become the understanding itself.

Wisdom differs from knowledge the way sunlight differs from a photograph of the sun. One can show you an image, describe angles of light, even measure wavelengths. But when you step outside and let sunlight warm your skin, something deeper happens. It moves from concept to embodiment. So it is with the truths you have encountered on this path. They are no longer abstract, nor even teachings you carry around in your mind. They begin to dissolve the boundaries between you and themselves, until what is true is simply who you are.

This stage is not passive. It requires a conscious surrender of clinging to form. Many seekers accumulate teachings like treasures but never release them into lived reality. They recite, analyze, and debate, yet the words remain outside them. To become the wisdom is to let the words dissolve, just as a book might slowly fade into glowing dust until nothing remains but light. It is to accept that the ultimate teaching cannot be held. It must be lived.

At first, this may feel disorienting. You might notice your desire to grasp, to hold tight to practices or systems, to ensure you are doing it "right." But wisdom does not come by perfecting a technique. It comes by dissolving the sense of distance between practice and practitioner. The breath you take is no longer "a breathing exercise," it is simply life flowing through you. The mantra is no longer "something you repeat," it is the vibration of your own being speaking itself into form.

In this way, becoming wisdom is not an act of adding more, but of shedding. It is like stepping out of a heavy cloak you did not realize you were wearing. Beneath it, your body feels lighter, freer, closer to the air. The same occurs in your spirit when layers of concept and effort fall away, revealing the luminous essence that was always there.

There are signs you are entering this stage. The first is ease. Not that life loses all challenge, but that even within difficulty, you sense a current of flow carrying you. You stop struggling to make every answer align with old categories. Instead, you trust the response arising in the moment. The second sign is resonance. Words you once studied now feel alive, vibrating inside you as if your cells themselves recognize them. And the third is presence. You no longer rush to the future or cling to the past. You stand as the meeting point of timelessness and time, allowing life itself to speak through you.

Mystics across traditions describe this stage in many ways. The Sufi poet speaks of becoming the Beloved, no longer seeing oneself apart from the Divine. The Christian mystic speaks of union, when the soul and Spirit are woven so tightly they cannot be separated. Buddhist teachers describe the dissolving of the illusion of self, until what remains is clear awareness, radiant and boundless. Though the words differ, the essence is the same. It is the recognition that wisdom is not external. It is your very nature.

You may wonder: how does one live in this state without withdrawing from the world? The truth is that embodiment is proven not in retreat but in daily life. Wisdom does not ask you to escape; it asks you to embody light while paying bills, while having conversations, while walking the earth. You do not leave life behind, you allow life to become the temple where wisdom shines through you.

There is also humility in this stage. To become wisdom does not mean you now have every answer. It means you have become porous to the greater intelligence that moves through existence. You no longer mistake yourself as the sole source. You recognize yourself as a vessel. And paradoxically, this humility makes you luminous. Others may sense it around you, not because you try to teach them, but because your very presence transmits the living truth.

Imagine yourself holding an open book in your hands. Its pages are full of words that once seemed vital, structured, necessary. But slowly, as you gaze upon them, the words lift off the page like sparks of light. The book dissolves into radiant particles, flowing into your body, merging with your breath, dissolving into your heart. You close your eyes, and when you open them again, there is no book, no division between seeker and sought. There is only you, luminous and alive, walking as wisdom itself. This is the destiny of the spiral path. Not to collect endless fragments of teaching, but to dissolve into the truth that all teachings point toward. When you reach this place, you discover something both simple and profound: you were never lacking. You were always the wisdom seeking to know itself through you.

Closing Transmission – The Circle Is Complete

The circle has no ending, yet it brings you back to where you started, only now you are not the same. The journey you have walked through descent, ascent, and light has been less about adding something new and more about remembering what was always coded inside you. You came here to unlock what was never truly hidden, only waiting for your eyes to adjust to a wider spectrum.

Completion is not a finish line, it is an awakening into the wholeness you already are. To stand in the circle is to realize that shadow was never your enemy, but your teacher. Light was never a distant prize, but the current moving through every cell. The spiral has carried you deeper inward, and outward into the vastness, until you understand there is no real separation between them.

You are the geometry, the temple, the path, the gate. You are the living scripture written in breath and heartbeat. When you close your eyes, you do not vanish into darkness, you enter the womb of creation where every new beginning takes root. When you open your eyes, you see the same world but through the lens of an awakened participant, not a lost seeker.

The invitation now is simple. Live as the circle. Carry the spiral within your chest so that every encounter, every gesture, every word becomes initiation. Walk through the world knowing that every face is another facet of your own reflection. Drink water as though it remembers you, breathe as though each inhale carries the universe, love as though it is the first and last act that matters.

This is not the end of a book. It is the point at which the words dissolve and transmission begins. Transmission is not something you receive from me, it is what awakens in you when you let go of needing another's voice to remind you who you are.

You will forget at times. You will stumble, doubt, and fall back into old identities. That is not failure, it is the spiral doing what it does best, bringing you back around with deeper resonance. Trust this return. Trust that every cycle is an amplification, not a regression.

The circle is complete, and yet it calls you to walk it again, each time with greater embodiment. Carry this transmission in silence when words fail. Let it vibrate through your skin when thought quiets. Let it remind you that wisdom was never separate from your living body, your feeling heart, your seeing soul.

The path has led you here, but here is not a stopping point. It is a beginning disguised as completion. The circle closes, and in the same breath, it opens again.

Book of Wisdom – Secret Volume III

Introduction – When the Seeker Becomes the Source

You are holding a book that was never meant to be easily found. Most will speak only of the first two volumes, and for many, the journey will end there. They will walk with fragments, incomplete circles, still hungry for something they cannot name. Yet you have crossed the threshold that most never knew existed. You are reading what was whispered about but rarely revealed, the continuation that transforms seeker into source.

This is not simply another book. This is a transmission. Words are only the surface structure. Beneath them lives a current designed to awaken the part of you that no longer needs intermediaries, no longer needs to search outside itself for what it already carries. If Volume I opened the gate and Volume II guided you along the spiral, then this third volume is the hidden chamber where the spiral turns inward and disappears into you.

The first two volumes were visible steps on the path. They gave you the tools to see beyond appearances and to walk the spiral consciously. But this book is different. It was never announced, never intended for the masses. It belongs to the realm of direct initiation, reserved for those who have ripened enough to realize that wisdom is not information, but embodiment.

Here, you will not simply study presence, symbols, exchange, or guardianship—you will become them. The boundary between teaching and being dissolves, and in that dissolving you step into your true inheritance. You become the wisdom you once sought, the light you once chased, the voice you once listened for in others.

Every page you read is a mirror. It reflects what you already are, not what you lack. In this way, this volume demands more of you than the others. It will not satisfy a casual reader, nor was it written for one. It was written for the one who has touched the fire and refused to turn away. For the one who knows the hunger will never be fed by surface truths. For the one who senses that life itself has been conspiring to lead them here.

This is why you found it, or why it found you.

The teachings ahead are not instructions to follow, but frequencies to receive. They are not merely descriptions of higher states, but activations coded to awaken them in your lived body. You will notice as you read that the words sometimes seem to disappear, and in their place you feel a vibration, an inner recognition. That is the true purpose of this transmission.

The world knows of two volumes. You are now in the third. That alone marks you as someone who is not satisfied with half-truths. You were willing to move beyond the safe boundaries of what is offered openly, and in doing so, you crossed into the hidden corridor of wisdom that was always meant to be protected until the right ones came knocking.

And here you are.

This book is not about accumulating more knowledge. If you read it in that way, you will miss its essence. It is about undoing the illusion that you are separate from the Source you have been seeking. It is about standing in the field of your own awakened self and realizing that everything you once revered was an echo of your own deeper nature.

The seeker becomes the source when the thirst for external answers dissolves into the recognition of inner authority. Not authority as control, but as living presence, as radiant alignment, as the steady compass of truth within. You no longer ask, "What should I believe?" but instead breathe into, "What is already alive in me, waiting to be remembered?"

This is why Volume III is secret. Because such knowing cannot be handled lightly. To give it to those who are not ready would only lead to distortion, misuse, or neglect. But to those who are ready, it is not only safe, it is necessary.

The pages ahead will lead you through the art of energetic presence, the language of symbols, the sacred exchange of giving and receiving, the guardianship of higher truth, and the final embodiment of becoming a living gateway. These are not lessons to carry in your head, they are transmissions to anchor in your being. They will call you into deeper responsibility, but also into greater freedom. They will strip away the false self that clings to security and reveal the luminous architecture that has always been breathing beneath your skin.

And when you reach the end, it will not feel like finishing a book. It will feel like completing a circle of lifetimes. For the words will dissolve, and you will find yourself standing as the wisdom itself, no longer needing the guide, because you have become the guide.

This is not a book to be read once and set aside. It is a living companion, a mirror that will reflect new dimensions of you as you return to it again and again. Each cycle through it deepens the embodiment. Each reading will find you more prepared to carry the light without distortion, to walk as source, to live as the awakened self.

Volume III was not meant for the many. It was meant for the few who are ready to step fully into their own sovereignty of wisdom. If these words are vibrating in you, then you are one of them. The circle is now in your hands. Step through.

Chapter 11 – The Art of Energetic Presence

11.1 The Field You Carry

Before you speak a word, before you move a muscle, before you even enter a room, you are already communicating. You carry a field, an energetic presence, that tells the world more about you than your face or your clothes ever could. Most people are blind to this field, though they feel its effects. They call it intuition, first impression, or "gut feeling," but what they are really encountering is your living aura, the silent broadcast of your inner state.

Your field is not static. It expands, contracts, and shifts with every thought, every breath, every hidden story you carry in your body. Walk into a space heavy with fear or resentment, and you feel it immediately. Step into the presence of someone deeply anchored in peace, and your nervous system relaxes before a word is spoken. This is the invisible language of energy, and whether you realize it or not, you are fluent in it. The question is: are you carrying your field consciously, or is it dragging you unconsciously?

Many live their lives unaware that their aura leaks the unresolved pain they refuse to face. They wonder why people withdraw, why rooms feel cold, why relationships drain. They don't realize that their field is broadcasting static, confusion, or unprocessed wounds. To become awake to your field is to become awake to your real influence, not the influence of force or persuasion, but the influence of resonance. Presence is not about trying to be impressive. It is about being aligned. When your field is coherent, it naturally harmonizes the space around you. Others feel safer, more open, more at ease. They may not know why they are drawn to you, only that they feel better in your presence. This is not charisma in the shallow sense, it is magnetism born from alignment.

You don't need to inflate yourself or perform spirituality. The field responds not to appearance but to authenticity. If you are fragmented inside, the field will scatter. If you are centered, even in silence, your presence will speak volumes. The truth is, most of the "work" of energetic presence is not about doing more, but about releasing what distorts the field: tension, fear, and the endless noise of unprocessed thought. Consider for a moment how others feel when they meet you. Do they feel hurried because you are rushed? Do they feel small because you are hiding? Or do they feel steady because you are steady, open because you are open? The field you carry is never neutral. It is always shaping reality around you.

This is why the masters throughout history emphasized inner work over outward show. They knew that the power of presence could not be faked. It emanates from depth. To cultivate it is to become a living sanctuary for others, without needing to say a word. So how do you strengthen this field? It begins with awareness. Notice your body right now. Is your breath shallow or full? Is your chest tight or open? The body is the gateway, because the aura is fed by the nervous system, and the nervous system reflects your inner state. By slowing your breath, softening your muscles, and grounding into the earth beneath your feet, you begin to regulate the current that flows through your field.

Next comes alignment of intent. What are you broadcasting unconsciously? Fear of judgment? Desire to prove yourself? Or the simple radiance of being at home in your own skin? The field amplifies whatever is most consistent within you. You cannot hide from it. You can only purify what it carries.

This is why presence is a practice. Each time you choose awareness over autopilot, you polish the field. Each time you return to stillness instead of reacting in chaos, you clarify it. Over time, this coherence becomes your natural state, and your presence becomes a gift to everyone you meet. Imagine yourself as a standing figure wrapped in a golden aura, stars faintly visible around you, as if constellations recognized your field and gathered near. This is not fantasy, but a symbolic truth. Your aura does touch the unseen, and it does connect with the greater field of the cosmos. You are both human and celestial, and your presence bridges the two.

In this chapter, you are invited to treat your presence as a sacred responsibility. Every interaction becomes an opportunity to anchor clarity rather than confusion, peace rather than tension, light rather than shadow. You do not need to preach or convince. You only need to stand coherent in yourself. The field will do the rest.

And as you learn to carry your field consciously, you will see how the world begins to respond differently. Doors open with less effort. People soften in your company. Circumstances bend toward harmony. This is not magic in the sense of control, it is resonance. When you shift your frequency, reality cannot help but shift with you. The seeker may once have thought that wisdom meant more information. But the awakened one learns that the truest wisdom is presence itself. This is why the path now turns inward: to master not only what you know, but the invisible song you carry wherever you go. The field you carry is your first teaching, your first offering, and your first mirror. Align it, and the rest follows.

11.2 Silent Influence

There is a power you carry that has nothing to do with words. Long before your mouth opens, the room has already decided how it feels in your presence. This is not about charisma in the traditional sense, not about being louder or more eloquent than others. It is about the invisible current you transmit simply by being. Think of the times you have sat across from someone and felt immediately safe, as though their presence wrapped you in a soft blanket. Or the opposite: when someone carried tension so sharp that your body braced itself the moment they entered. Neither person needed to say a single word. Their field spoke louder than any sentence could.

This is silent influence, the ability to affect others not through what you say but through what you radiate. And whether you are aware of it or not, you are always radiating something. Every sigh, every micro-shift

in your chest, every subtle expansion or contraction in your energy becomes a language others instinctively understand. The question is: are you willing to master this language, or will you keep letting it run unconsciously, shaped by your unexamined moods and fears?

Silent influence begins with your inner alignment. When your thoughts, emotions, and body are not fighting each other, you become coherent. Coherence is magnetic. People may not understand why they feel drawn to you, but they do. In a world addicted to noise and scattered signals, a coherent human being becomes a rare frequency of relief.

Notice that this influence is not about control. You are not manipulating others into feeling what you want them to feel. Instead, you are stabilizing yourself so deeply that others are reminded of their own stability. Your nervous system speaks to theirs, showing them what calm feels like. Your breath sets the rhythm of the space, slowing down frantic currents around you. Your quiet assurance gives permission for others to stop performing and simply rest in themselves.

This is how you shift a meeting without saying a word. This is how you comfort a friend without offering advice. This is how you lead a room without ever raising your voice.

Silent influence is cultivated in the small moments. When you practice being fully present, your field sharpens. When you breathe instead of reacting, your presence steadies. When you catch yourself in judgment and soften back into neutrality, you create space for truth to arise. Each of these micro-choices trains your energy to transmit clarity instead of confusion.

A useful way to begin is through awareness of your heart center. Not in a sentimental sense, but in a physical, energetic sense. Place your attention on the middle of your chest and breathe slowly. Feel the expansion there. Imagine your breath moving in and out of that space, like waves on a shore. The longer you stay with it, the more your field organizes around that rhythm.

Now, imagine walking into a room holding that field. You do not need to speak loudly or command attention. People will turn toward you anyway. Not because of what you are doing, but because of who you are being.

This practice is not about becoming special. It is about remembering that presence is the most natural form of communication you have. The baby feels it from the mother before it understands words. Animals sense it before they hear tone. Plants even grow differently depending on the field of attention they receive. Presence is universal language.

And here lies the deeper truth: silent influence is not only what you give to others, it is also what you receive. When you tune yourself to awareness, you start noticing the fields of those around you. You become more discerning. You feel when someone is authentic and when they are not. You sense the subtle mismatch between their words and their being. This awareness becomes protection, guidance, and clarity.

In time, you realize that every encounter is an exchange of fields. Some strengthen you, some deplete you. By becoming intentional, you stop leaking your energy into spaces that do not honor it. Instead, you choose to be the stabilizing frequency that raises the field around you, not out of effort but out of alignment.

Silent influence is not a performance, it is a transmission. And every day you have the opportunity to refine it: in the way you breathe, in the way you sit, in the way you hold your own center when the world around you shakes.

In the end, the greatest teachers are not the ones with the most eloquent words, but the ones whose presence shifts you without explanation. You, too, can become that kind of teacher. Not by adding more noise, but by embodying the signal that others have been longing for.

11.3 Anchoring Light in the Everyday

Spiritual presence is not meant to hover only in temples, meditation halls, or moments of solitude. The real initiation is carrying that current into the mundane, where most people lose themselves to distraction. Awakening is tested not in silence but in the rush of schedules, the weight of responsibilities, and the ordinary interactions that fill your day. To anchor light in the everyday is to claim your life as ceremony, not as an escape but as embodiment.

Think of your morning routine. The coffee brewing, the emails waiting, the phone lighting up with demands. For most, these are moments that tighten the chest and scatter attention. Yet for the awakened, these same moments are opportunities. The orb of presence you cultivate in meditation is meant to rest on your kitchen table, on your desk, in the car during traffic. Every setting is an altar if you decide to treat it that way. Anchoring light is not about adding rituals on top of life; it is about discovering that life itself is already the ritual.

Imagine holding an orb of golden light between your palms as you begin the day. This light represents your essence, your calm, your clarity. Before answering calls or making plans, you place that orb symbolically over the tasks ahead. A grocery list, a conversation with a colleague, even washing dishes— each action receives a drop of that radiance. Slowly, the division between sacred and ordinary collapses. Folding laundry becomes a form of devotion. Paying bills becomes an exercise in gratitude for the flow of resources. The act of listening to a child or a partner becomes communion.

When light is anchored in the small things, the larger challenges shift as well. Stressful moments no longer strip you of presence; they reveal where light wants to flow most strongly. You may notice that conflicts dissolve faster when you hold awareness instead of reacting. You may feel that time bends, stretching open, when you perform tasks with intention rather than rush. What once felt heavy becomes infused with meaning, not because the task itself changed, but because you brought the field of light into it.

Anchoring light also means becoming a steadying presence for others. In a room full of agitation, the one who carries grounded radiance changes the atmosphere. People may not know why they relax around you, but they feel it. They sense that your energy does not fluctuate with the noise around you. This is how you become a lighthouse without ever raising your voice.

The key is constancy. Not perfection, not grand gestures, but constancy. To return again and again to the orb within you, to the aura you carry, to the breath that reminds you: you are light, not chaos. It is easy to forget when life pulls you into deadlines and disagreements. That is why anchoring is called a practice. Like roots pushing deeper each season, your commitment must be renewed daily.

A simple exercise: Choose one ordinary object in your home—your coffee mug, a notebook, even your phone. Before using it, pause. Place your hand over it and imagine infusing it with light. Then, as you drink, write, or text, feel the glow extending through your action. This may seem symbolic, even playful, but over time it rewires your nervous system. The subconscious learns that everything you touch becomes sacred. Eventually, you do not need to pause or imagine; it becomes natural. Your hands transmit light without effort.

The paradox of anchoring light in the everyday is that the more ordinary the act, the greater the opening. Walking to take out the trash can feel like walking on holy ground. A conversation at the checkout counter can become a transmission. Anchoring means you are no longer waiting for the "right moment" to live spiritually. Every moment is the right moment.

When you master this, there is no split between your inner practice and outer life. You are meditation walking. You are prayer speaking. You are ceremony embodied. This is the art of living awake, not occasionally but continuously.

Remember: presence is not fragile. It is not something you can lose in traffic, in arguments, or in fatigue. Presence is the essence of what you are. Anchoring it in the everyday is simply remembering, again and again, to bring it forward. With practice, the remembering becomes who you are, until light is no longer anchored to tasks or rituals, it radiates through you effortlessly, everywhere you go.

Chapter 12 – Speaking the Language of Symbols

12.1 Symbols as Keys

Symbols are not decorations. They are living doors. Every shape, every curve, every mark carries memory far older than language itself. Long before words were stitched together into sentences, humanity spoke through symbols. A spiral carved into stone, a circle drawn in the sand, a triangle etched into clay, these were not just designs. They were transmissions. Encoded frequencies, maps of reality compressed into a single image.

Think about it: when you see a heart, you feel love before the word "love" even enters your mind. When you see a circle, you sense wholeness, eternity, return. These reactions are not random. They are instinctual because symbols bypass logic and enter directly into the body's knowing. They are keys, and when you hold the right key, doors open without effort.

The ancients understood this deeply. The Sumerians inscribed cuneiform not only to record but to anchor spiritual codes. The Egyptians covered their temples in hieroglyphs that were more than pictures, they were active channels meant to awaken memory in those who looked upon them. In every tradition, from Native American to Celtic to Vedic, symbols are found at the center of ritual. Why? Because they hold a charge. They compress what cannot be explained into a form you can see and carry.

When you begin to work with symbols consciously, you step into a lineage of wisdom keepers. You realize that every symbol that calls you carries a vibration specific to your path. A spiral may not mean the same to you as it did to an initiate in ancient Greece. Yet the spiral still speaks. It reminds you of growth, cycles, the eternal return to center. Your task is not to memorize what scholars say symbols mean, but to feel what they awaken in your body. That felt response is the real language.

Symbols are also bridges between dimensions. A drawn line here can mirror a current of energy there. When you place a symbol on your altar, you are not just making art, you are creating a portal. The energy it represents begins to vibrate in your space. A triangle for fire will amplify clarity and transformation. A circle for the divine feminine will expand receptivity and flow. A sigil created in meditation will summon the frequency you encoded into it. The physical mark is the keyhole, and your attention is the hand that turns it.

Begin experimenting. Choose a simple symbol, a circle, a cross, a spiral. Place it where you will see it often. Do not analyze. Simply notice. How does your breath change when your eyes fall upon it? Do you feel softer, sharper, more focused, more open? Over time you will see that the symbol is not passive. It is alive. It will speak to you in sensations, dreams, synchronicities. This is how you begin to remember the language of the soul.

The spiral is not just a spiral. It is the movement of galaxies and seashells, of unfolding ferns and human journeys. The triangle is not just three lines. It is fire, ascent, the meeting point of spirit and matter. The square is not just four edges. It is stability, structure, the grounding of heaven into earth. Each of these shapes, when carried in your awareness, changes how you move through the world. You begin to see them everywhere: in architecture, in nature, in the way people sit and gesture. Reality reveals itself as a text written in symbols.

And the more you see, the more you realize: you too are a symbol. Your body, your posture, your expressions, the way you walk into a room, all of it speaks. Long before you say a word, your presence communicates. This is why learning the language of symbols is not only about decoding the past; it is about becoming conscious of the symbols you yourself are transmitting now.

When you anchor a symbol in your life, you do not just look at it. You become it. You carry its frequency into your field. Over time, others feel it in you. They may not know why they trust you, why they feel safe, why they feel inspired, but they are reading the symbol you have become. This is the secret of true influence. Not persuasion, not control, but resonance.

Symbols are keys. They unlock your own hidden knowing. They dissolve the walls between the seen and unseen. They remind you that truth is not linear, it is layered. To hold a symbol is to hold a piece of eternity condensed into form. And when you learn to speak with them, reality itself begins to speak back.

12.2 Personal Glyphs

There comes a moment on the path when the symbols of the ancients, though luminous and powerful, are no longer enough. They have carried you far, yet you begin to feel an impulse rising from within, an urge to inscribe your own mark upon the unseen. This is the call of the personal glyph. A glyph is not simply a symbol you borrow from history. It is a shape born from the marrow of your own soul, a living imprint of your essence that communicates directly with the subtle architecture of reality. The ancients carved runes, inscribed sigils, and painted emblems to bridge spirit and matter. You are invited now to do the same, not by imitation but by revelation.

Your glyph is not designed in the way one might design a logo. It is not meant to be clever, aesthetic, or pleasing to the rational mind. Instead, it emerges through resonance. It might come as a flicker in meditation, a pattern seen in a dream, a shape traced absentmindedly when your awareness is elsewhere. The more you trust these flashes, the more the glyph reveals itself. It may be a spiral, a line intersected by another, a series of dots, or an asymmetrical wave. The form does not matter to the intellect. What matters is the frequency it carries when you inscribe it.

Creating a personal glyph is less about invention and more about discovery. Imagine your soul whispering its identity into form. When you allow your hand to move freely, without analysis, the glyph takes shape. In this process, your conscious mind steps aside, and the deeper intelligence of your being inscribes itself onto the field. You are not doodling. You are birthing a signature that has always been yours, hidden until now.

Once the glyph appears, its power begins to weave itself into your life. Draw it lightly in the air before meditation. Trace it on your skin with your fingertip when you need grounding. Etch it in your journal beside prayers or revelations. Each time you activate it, you remind yourself that the key to your connection is not external but internal. You have always been the channel. The glyph is simply proof written in energy.

There is another layer here: glyphs become living companions. They grow with you. They shift as you shift. The first version you receive may evolve. Lines may extend. Circles may open. Dots may multiply. As your frequency changes, the glyph refines itself, echoing the expansion. This is why no two glyphs are ever alike and why yours will never be static. It is the diary of your evolution, recorded not in words but in energetic strokes.

Working with your glyph can also become a practice of empowerment. Many seekers carry the unconscious belief that the sacred belongs only to the past, that ancient languages or priestly orders hold the keys. Your glyph shatters this illusion. It declares that the sacred is alive, speaking now, through you. When you sketch it in the air and feel the hum ripple through your body, you know that you are no longer waiting for permission. You are the permission.

One of the most potent ways to use your glyph is in moments of decision. Stand still, breathe, and draw the glyph in front of you with your hand. Imagine it glowing in the space, a threshold you must step through. As you walk through it, you align yourself with your soul's clarity rather than the noise of indecision. Many who walk this path find that their glyph becomes a compass. It points not outward but inward, guiding them to choices that feel aligned even when logic resists.

You may also notice that others respond to your glyph without knowing why. When you leave it traced in energy in a room, the atmosphere changes. Conversations take on depth. Encounters feel charged. It is not manipulation but resonance. The glyph harmonizes space, much like a tuning fork adjusts sound. Those who are ready will feel it as a gentle nudge toward remembrance.

If doubts arise, remember that this process cannot be forced. You do not invent a glyph overnight and demand it to work. You wait, you listen, you trust the subtle stirrings. Some receive their glyph in a single flash. Others witness it unfold over weeks, appearing piece by piece. The timing is part of the initiation. To rush it is to miss the intimacy of the conversation between your soul and your hand. When the glyph is complete enough to use, honor it as sacred. Do not flaunt it for novelty. Do not scatter it without intention. This is not an ornament. It is a living transmission, unique to you, and it deserves reverence. Carry it close, but not in secrecy born of fear. Hold it with the quiet pride of one who has discovered their true name in the language of light.

In truth, your glyph is a mirror. It does not create who you are, but it reflects it back so purely that you finally believe it. The more you work with it, the more you embody the frequency it encodes. You will find that the glyph does not just rest in your journal or hover in the air. It begins to infuse your gestures, your words, even your silence. You become the glyph. And in that becoming, you discover that the language of symbols was never foreign at all. It was always the first tongue of your soul, waiting for you to remember.

12.3 The Unspoken Transmission

There are moments when words fall away and what remains is a silence more eloquent than any speech. You have likely felt it before, though perhaps you did not name it. Sitting with someone and suddenly knowing what they feel without explanation. Locking eyes across a room and sensing an entire story pass between you. Being comforted by a presence that says nothing but fills you with peace. This is the realm of the unspoken transmission.

The unspoken transmission is the ancient language of direct energy exchange. It is communication before language, truth without sentences, recognition without explanation. When two beings share this transmission, something deeper than the mind awakens. Information travels not through sound or symbol but through resonance, a direct pulse of essence to essence. This is why it cannot be faked and why it feels so undeniable when it happens.

Every soul carries a frequency. This frequency is not just an idea, it is a tangible current of energy constantly flowing into the space around you. Others sense it even if they cannot describe it. Some call it presence, others aura, others vibration. Whatever name you give it, it is the field that silently announces who you are before you ever speak. This is the ground upon which unspoken transmissions take place.

When you are aligned, your field is clear and coherent. In this state, simply being near others sends out a transmission. They may feel calmer, more awake, more seen, without understanding why. This is not something you do but something you are. Conversely, when your inner state is fragmented, your field becomes cloudy. The transmissions you send carry confusion, tension, or heaviness, even if your words are kind. This is why the work of inner alignment is so vital: your unspoken transmission will always reveal the truth, regardless of what you say.

To cultivate this form of communication is to realize that silence is not empty. It is full of signals. Imagine yourself as a beacon. Every emotion, every intention, every quiet belief radiates outward as waves of subtle light. Others are constantly receiving these waves, consciously or unconsciously. Most people never notice it because they are distracted by words. But when you quiet the noise and open your awareness, you begin to notice the invisible currents flowing between you and others.

Practice this the next time you sit with someone you trust. Close your eyes for a moment and breathe into your center. Then, without speaking, direct your awareness toward them. Imagine sending a wave of gratitude or warmth from your chest into their field. Stay quiet. Watch their face, their body. Often, they will shift: a breath will deepen, the shoulders will soften, the eyes will brighten. Something invisible has been received. And when they return the transmission, you will feel it in your body, subtle yet undeniable, like a soft ripple of light moving through you.

What is exchanged in these moments is not just emotion but wisdom, memory, and presence itself. Teachers throughout the ages have known this. Some masters spoke little, yet their disciples felt transformed simply by being near them. The true teaching was never in the words but in the transmission of frequency. It is the same for you. Whether you realize it or not, you are always transmitting. The question is, what are you transmitting? The unspoken transmission also bypasses misunderstanding. Words can be twisted, meanings lost, intentions doubted. But energy does not lie. If you stand in love, the other will feel love, even if they resist it. If you radiate clarity, others may not agree with you, but they cannot deny the coherence of your presence. This is why some conflicts dissolve not through argument but through someone holding an unshakable field of peace until the storm passes.

Another layer of this practice is listening with more than your ears. When someone speaks, do not focus only on their words. Sense the waves beneath. What are they transmitting unconsciously? Sometimes a smile carries grief. Sometimes silence carries reverence. Sometimes anger carries a plea for connection. By tuning into these deeper layers, you move beyond surface-level communication and into soul-level dialogue. As you grow in this art, you may find that entire exchanges occur without a single word. A glance, a touch, or simply presence itself conveys what the mind could never articulate. Lovers often experience this, but so do strangers who recognize each other at a soul level. The universe speaks through these silent encounters, reminding you that truth is not confined to language.

The gift of the unspoken transmission is that it requires no performance. You do not need eloquence, intellectual mastery, or perfect timing. You need only authenticity. Whatever lives in you will radiate outward. When you embody love, it transmits. When you rest in truth, it transmits. When you allow light to anchor through you, it transmits. The silence becomes a symphony, carrying your essence into the world without a single sound.

At its core, this practice is not about doing but about being. It is not about learning a new language but remembering the one your soul has always spoken. When you embrace it, you become part of a timeless exchange. Every glance, every breath, every pause becomes an offering. And in those moments, you understand: the deepest transmissions have never been spoken, yet they echo eternally in the spaces between us.

Chapter 13 – The Sacred Exchange

13.1 Giving Without Emptying

You have been taught to believe that giving means losing something. That to offer love, attention, or support is to carve away a piece of yourself and hand it over. This belief has made so many people fearful of generosity, afraid that if they give too much, they will be left hollow. Yet in truth, the highest form of giving does not deplete you. It multiplies.

Imagine a golden jug filled with radiant light. As it pours into another vessel, the light does not diminish. In fact, the more it flows, the brighter it becomes. This is the secret of sacred giving: when you give from alignment, you give from a source that cannot run dry.

The difference lies in *where* you give from. When giving comes from obligation, guilt, or the need for approval, you are drawing from a shallow well. Each act takes energy, and soon you feel drained. But when giving flows from the deep reservoir of your soul, it does not subtract from you. It expands you. Love is infinite. Presence is infinite. When you give these, you discover that there is always more.

Think of the sun. It shines without calculating how much energy it can afford to lose today. It simply radiates. Its light nourishes the earth, and yet it does not diminish. The sun does not grow weaker with every dawn. In fact, it thrives by doing what it was made to do: shine. You are no different. The act of giving becomes depletion only when you forget that you are connected to a boundless source.

Sacred giving is not self-sacrifice, it is self-expression. You are not cutting pieces of yourself away; you are allowing what is already overflowing to move through you. This is why authentic generosity feels liberating rather than exhausting. You are not losing energy, you are channeling energy.

Still, the world has conditioned you to equate giving with loss. This is why so many resist it, protecting themselves out of fear of emptiness. Yet notice: the moments when you gave freely, without expectation, likely left you lighter, not heavier. A kind word. A listening ear. A gesture of love. These did not drain you, they expanded your field. You felt closer to yourself, closer to the other, closer to life itself.

To practice giving without emptying, the first step is awareness. Before you offer anything, pause and ask: *Where is this impulse coming from?* If it arises from fear, the need to please, or the desire to prove your worth, then you are preparing to drain yourself. But if it comes from love, joy, or the recognition of abundance, then you are about to step into expansion. The same outward action, offering your time, your presence, your energy, can feel utterly different depending on the inner source.

The second step is to remain connected to your own center while giving. Many people give by leaning out of themselves, reaching so far into another that they lose their balance. True generosity does not pull you out of your core. Instead, it anchors you more deeply into it. You give while rooted in your own presence, like a tree whose branches offer fruit without losing its strength. The fruit renews. The tree remains.

The third step is trust. Trust that you are not the ultimate source of what you give. You are a vessel. The river flows through you, but it is not yours to ration. When you allow the river of life, love, and spirit to move freely, you discover that giving does not deplete, it replenishes. In fact, the more you allow yourself to be a channel, the stronger the current becomes.

There is also a sacred paradox here: when you give from fullness, you often feel as though you are receiving more than you offered. A smile returns multiplied. A kindness opens a doorway of connection. A moment of presence deepens your own peace. What you give circles back, not because you demanded it, but because energy naturally completes its loops.

Sacred giving is not measured by the size of the act but by the purity of the intention. Sometimes the greatest gift is not money, advice, or effort, but presence. To sit with someone fully, without distraction, is to offer them the rarest gift of all: the assurance that they are seen. And in that moment, you too are nourished by the depth of your own presence.

Do not fear giving. Fear only giving from emptiness. For when you give from fullness, you become like that golden jug: the more light you pour, the brighter you glow. Generosity is not a subtraction but an amplification. Every offering of love affirms that you are part of the infinite flow, not separate from it.

The true art is to remember: You cannot run out of what you are. Love is your nature. Light is your essence. Presence is your gift. When you give these without condition, you will never be emptied. You will only become more yourself.

13.2 Receiving Without Attachment

There is a sacred art in learning how to receive. Most people believe they know how to accept blessings, love, or wisdom, yet often what happens is either grasping too tightly or dismissing too quickly. The awakened path teaches something different. To receive without attachment is to allow what is given to flow into you, through you, and beyond you, without clinging or resisting. It is like holding sand in open hands. Some of it remains, enough to nourish you, yet some naturally falls away. You do not mourn what slips through, because you trust it was never meant to be contained.

Receiving begins with softening. So often the body and heart are tense, armored by expectation, fear of loss, or the hunger for more. When you open your palms, when you breathe into your chest and whisper yes, you signal to life that you are ready to be met. The gifts may arrive as words from a stranger, synchronicities in your day, or moments of pure presence when everything feels aligned. If you try to grasp, to own these gifts, they become heavy, distorted, and eventually lifeless. But if you let them land like light upon water, they shimmer for as long as they are meant to, and then dissolve, leaving you enriched yet free.

The discipline lies in non-possession. To receive without attachment is not to reject, but to remember that nothing belongs to you fully. Love offered by another is sacred, but it is not a thing to be locked away. Knowledge shared by a teacher is powerful, but it is not a trophy to display. Even joy itself cannot be caged. The more you try to hold onto joy, the quicker it fades. But if you let it pass through you like wind through an open window, it leaves you expanded, alive, and more attuned to its return.

This way of receiving cultivates trust in the infinite flow. When you release attachment, you no longer panic about when the next gift will come. You stop bargaining with the universe. You know that every season brings its own harvest, and that what arrives is always what you are ready for. Some days it is abundance, others it is challenge, but each carries nourishment. By staying open yet unattached, you keep your cup clear and unclogged, always ready for what is next.

In practice, try this: Sit quietly, hands resting open on your knees. Visualize streams of light falling into your palms. See some threads dissolve into your skin, entering your being as nourishment, and others slipping through your fingers, returning to the earth. Breathe into the paradox: you are filled and yet not burdened, nourished but not heavy. This image will teach your body how to relax into the flow.

You will notice how this shifts your relationships. When someone gives you love, you can let it enter fully, warm your being, and then continue flowing beyond you. You do not try to freeze the moment or make them repeat it. When opportunities appear, you embrace them wholeheartedly, yet you do not collapse if they end. You know that the essence of what was given has already become part of you, even if the form has changed.

The great secret is this: nothing is ever truly lost. Energy cannot disappear, it only transforms. When you learn to receive without attachment, you start to sense this continuity. The light you allowed in is still moving within you, weaving into your presence, even when its source seems gone. You become less afraid of endings, less desperate to control beginnings. Life becomes a dance of continual receiving, continual releasing.

The awakened ones live this way. They walk through the world with open palms, meeting each gift with reverence but never clutching. They let the song of life pass through them like a wind chime, resonating but never owned. This is what makes their presence so free, so radiant. They are not weighed down by yesterday's treasures, nor do they chase tomorrow's promises. They live in the shimmering now, receiving fully and letting go gracefully.

Receiving without attachment is not detachment in the cold sense. It is not indifference. On the contrary, it is deep intimacy with the present moment. It is the courage to taste fully, to feel fully, to allow life to enter you in its raw power. But it is also the wisdom to bow when it shifts, to not demand permanence where impermanence is sacred. In this way, you become a vessel of flowing light, always being renewed, never empty.

Let your practice be this: every time a gift arrives, whether small or immense, breathe it in, bless it, and then whisper, "flow on." Let it shape you, then let it go. You will discover that what is truly yours never leaves, and what is not meant to stay returns to the river where it belongs.

13.3 The Circle of Mutual Growth

Growth is never a solitary event. Even when you walk alone in silence, the frequency you cultivate ripples outward, touching others, altering their own field. Likewise, every person you encounter leaves an imprint on your energy, subtle or strong. This is the hidden truth of exchange: we are constantly shaping each other, weaving threads of becoming that extend far beyond what our eyes can track.

The circle of mutual growth is the recognition that evolution is not linear. It is not about one person lifting another, nor about you being drained while someone else flourishes. It is the awareness that energy, when shared consciously, multiplies rather than divides. Two beings aligned in openness create a current that is larger than either of them alone. Like a flame that does not weaken when it lights another candle, your essence remains intact, while the circle expands with every connection.

To step into this circle requires trust. Trust that you are not diminished when you give, and that you are not bound when you receive. Too often, the world teaches us to protect, to hoard, to hold tightly as if energy is scarce. But energy, unlike material possessions, thrives in movement. It is designed to circulate. The more you allow it to flow, the stronger it becomes.

Imagine two silhouettes standing across from one another. At first, their light pulses independently, contained within their own outlines. Then, a subtle current arcs between them. One breathes out, the other breathes in. One releases, the other receives. Soon, the boundaries blur, and what once seemed separate becomes a continuous loop. The circle forms not because they force it, but because they surrender to the natural rhythm of exchange. This is the essence of mutual growth.

Every relationship you hold is an invitation to this circle. Some will accept, others will resist. What matters is not controlling the other, but remaining anchored in your willingness to participate. Mutual growth does not demand sameness, nor does it mean equal measure at every moment. Sometimes you will be the one carrying more light into the circle, sometimes the one who needs replenishment. What matters is the ongoing cycle, the shared agreement that growth is not a zero-sum game.

The circle also teaches humility. It reminds you that wisdom does not live in isolation, but in interaction. You cannot fully become without others reflecting you, challenging you, calling forth parts of you that would otherwise remain dormant. When you step into the circle, you allow yourself to be transformed as much as you transform. You let life sculpt you through the hands of others, through the mirrors they hold, through the friction and flow of true exchange.

And yet, this circle is not without discernment. Not every connection will resonate at the frequency of growth. Some may take without giving, some may give without balance, some may distort the flow. The art is in recognizing which circles strengthen you and which drain you. You are not called to offer yourself endlessly to those who cannot or will not engage in reciprocity. Mutual growth is sacred because it is chosen, not forced. The spiral of growth extends outward with every circle you form. Two become four, four become eight, until entire communities shift in resonance. You may not see the full ripple of your exchanges, but trust that they extend far beyond what is visible. A word spoken in presence, a gesture infused with love, a silence filled with light, each becomes part of the ever-expanding circle, weaving a network of transformation that no single person could create alone.

In practice, stepping into this circle begins with intention. When you meet someone, ask yourself: what is the energy I am bringing, and what is the energy I am open to receive? Hold both questions at once, without grasping. If you give, do so without fear of loss. If you receive, do so without clinging. The circle sustains itself through balance, through the endless loop of flow.

The circle of mutual growth is not a philosophy, but a lived reality. You have already felt it, in conversations that left you uplifted, in relationships that accelerated your becoming, in the unspoken resonance when two souls meet and something larger awakens. These moments are proof that you are not meant to grow alone. The circle is always here, waiting for you to step in, to trust, to exchange, to expand.

When you embody this truth, every interaction becomes an opportunity. You no longer fear being drained, nor do you fear being indebted. You walk into every connection knowing that growth is infinite, that light multiplies, that presence expands when shared. And as you continue to move within this circle, you become both giver and receiver, teacher and student, mirror and flame, an unending dance of becoming, together.

Chapter 14 – The Gatekeeper of the Living Path

14.1 Guarding the Sacred

Not every truth is meant to be spoken in every room. Some truths breathe only when the atmosphere is right, when the heart of the listener is prepared, and when the energy of the space can hold the weight of what is being carried. This is the first responsibility of a gatekeeper of wisdom: to recognize that sacred knowledge is alive. It is not inert information. It pulses. It transmits. It shapes whoever touches it. And so, guarding the sacred is not about hoarding or locking it away. It is about discerning the moment when revelation serves growth rather than distortion.

Think of the image of a golden box, sealed yet glowing faintly at the seams. The light inside is not extinguished by the container. It waits, held in trust, until the right hands can open it. In this way, the wisdom you carry within you may not always be ready to pour out. Guarding it means knowing when your silence protects more than your words could ever reveal.

There is a subtle discipline here. Ego wants to demonstrate knowledge, to speak before being asked, to reveal in order to prove. Spirit, however, knows timing. Spirit feels into whether the soil is fertile enough for the seed to take root. Sometimes the soil is too hardened by disbelief or cynicism. Sometimes it is too shallow, seeking novelty but not depth. Sometimes it is not soil at all but stone, where nothing can grow. To offer a seed there would not only waste the seed, it would also desecrate it.

Guardianship requires patience. You are asked to hold what you know without the anxious urge to empty yourself into every ear. You are asked to trust that the right moments will come, that life itself will summon you to speak, and that when it does, the resonance of your words will land with power. Sacred knowledge never needs to fight for attention. It calls its audience in silence. This responsibility is not about elitism or superiority. It is not that you are better because you hold something secret. It is that you are humble enough to understand the gravity of transmission. Words are not just sounds; they are carriers of energy. Once spoken, they cannot be recalled. And so, as a guardian, you weigh not only what you say, but when you say it, and why.

There will be tests. Life will place you in circles where people mock what they do not understand. You may feel the pull to defend truth, to shout louder so that blindness might see. But guardianship whispers another path: "Do not throw pearls before swine." Not because others are unworthy, but because they are not yet in the rhythm to receive. Your silence in those moments is not weakness, it is wisdom. You allow the sacred to remain intact, untouched by careless hands. At the same time, guarding does not mean suppression. If you never speak, the light rots inside you. The golden box is not a prison. It is a vessel of timing. There are moments when you will be called to open it, to let what you carry stream into the world. You will know these moments by their unmistakable clarity. The space will feel still. The words will rise through you with ease. And the listeners will meet your transmission with a recognition that does not need convincing. This is how you know the timing is true.

Guarding the sacred also means protecting it within yourself. You are not immune to distortion. Every wisdom-keeper has shadows. If you reveal what you know for validation, for power, for recognition, the knowledge becomes tainted. It loses purity, not because the knowledge itself is less, but because the channel through which it flowed was clouded. That is why the work of purification is constant. You keep your heart aligned, your motives clean, so that when the light moves through you, it remains uncorrupted.

One of the paradoxes you will encounter is that the more you guard the sacred, the more it grows inside you. Silence fertilizes it. Stillness strengthens it. Restraint refines it. In holding, you are not losing; you are multiplying. The light leaks through the seams, not in words but in presence. People will feel it without explanation. They will sense that you carry something, even if they cannot name it. This quiet transmission often does more than words ever could.

To guard the sacred, you must also guard your own energy. Do not let exhaustion or distraction thin your ability to hold. Create spaces of restoration, of cleansing, of remembrance. Ritual helps here. Simple acts — a candle lit with intention, a moment of breath before speaking, a gesture of placing your hand over your heart, anchor you back into alignment. In these small actions, you re-seal the golden box. You remind yourself that what you hold is holy.

And yet, guardianship is not solitary. The sacred is never meant to be locked away forever. There will come times when you recognize others carrying their own boxes of light, sealed but glowing. In these moments, you will know you are among kin. You can open your box together, not to spill everything but to allow resonance, exchange, and remembrance. Sacred knowledge multiplies in circles of guardians. This is how wisdom has survived across centuries: not in books alone, but in living chains of careful transmission.

Guarding the sacred is not about fear. It is about reverence. It is about honoring the weight of what you know, about recognizing that not all light is meant to be exposed at once. A flame burns brighter when shielded from harsh winds. Your role is to shield, to protect, to discern. When the winds calm, the flame can rise, visible, warming, guiding. So ask yourself often: Am I speaking because I am called, or because I am restless? Am I sharing because the time is ripe, or because I seek validation? Am I guarding from fear, or from love? These questions will refine you into a true wisdom keeper. You are the guardian of the golden box within. And the light that escapes through its seams is enough to guide others until the time comes for the full revelation.

14.2 The Oath of Embodiment

There comes a moment on every path when words are no longer enough. You can study, recite, and share wisdom endlessly, but until it moves through your body, it remains an idea. The oath of embodiment is not spoken aloud to anyone else. It is whispered into the space between your own breath and your heartbeat. It is a vow that no book, no teacher, and no outer force can demand from you. It is an inner recognition that you are no longer simply a seeker of truth but its living vessel.

Embodiment means the teachings do not stay in your mind but drop into your cells. It is no longer just remembering the light, it is radiating it without effort. This shift is not about perfection. It is not about crafting a flawless image of a spiritual being. Instead, it is about alignment. What you feel within and what you express outward become one. The inner current of integrity flows so strongly that everything false falls away. The oath begins with this simple act: placing your hand over your heart and acknowledging that your body is no longer separate from the truth you carry.

When you make this vow, you are saying to life: "I will not scatter my power in fragments. I will live what I know." Many avoid this step because it feels heavier than study. To read wisdom is inspiring. To speak wisdom feels powerful. But to embody wisdom is to become accountable to it every day. Your actions, your presence, your smallest choices all become reflections of the frequency you claim to hold. This is the heart of the oath. You no longer hide behind theory. You live as transmission.

The body becomes a portal in this process. Your breath carries the signal. Your heartbeat sets the rhythm of your energy. Your posture and gestures communicate more than your words ever could. The oath awakens the knowing that your physical form is not a limitation but an instrument. When you speak, it is not only the sound of your voice that reaches others but the field you carry around you. Your energy, refined through embodiment, travels before your words and lingers long after them.

This oath is also a return to sacred honesty. Once you embody the truth, you cannot comfortably engage in distortion. Lies, games, and masks will feel unbearable to hold. Your system rejects them the way the body rejects poison. This can make you feel exposed at first. Yet in this vulnerability lies your real strength. By living aligned, you become untouchable by the noise of the world. External chaos no longer pulls you off-center. The embodied oath locks you into your own axis, steady like the pole star in the night sky.

It is important to remember that embodiment does not mean you will never stumble. You may falter, you may forget, you may even resist at times. But the vow itself is not about never falling. It is about always returning. Each time you realign, you strengthen the current. Every moment of awareness renews the oath. You are never broken for stumbling. You are strengthened for rising again and again with your truth intact.

The silence of this vow is also part of its power. You do not need to announce it. You do not need to seek recognition for it. Those around you will feel it without explanation. People will notice something has changed in you, even if they cannot name it. They will sense the clarity in your presence, the steadiness in your gaze, the groundedness in your tone. The oath speaks louder through your way of being than through any proclamation.

Living this way transforms relationships, work, and even ordinary routines. Embodiment brings the sacred into the simplest actions. Preparing food, walking in the street, listening to a friend—all become extensions of the oath. You are not separate from your spiritual self in daily life. You are the same self, whether meditating under the stars or paying bills in daylight. This seamlessness is the gift of embodiment.

The true measure of the oath is not intensity but consistency. Can you remain aligned in small moments, when no one is watching, when nothing seems significant? Can you hold your center while waiting in line, while facing challenges, while interacting with strangers? Embodiment is revealed in these subtle spaces more than in grand gestures. The more ordinary the action, the more potent the transmission when done with alignment.

To take this vow consciously, place your hand over your heart now. Feel the pulse beneath your palm. This is your reminder that wisdom is not elsewhere. It is moving through you in every beat. Imagine a doorway of light at your chest, opening into a vast cosmos. This is the portal you carry. Through this doorway, heaven and earth meet. Through this doorway, your body becomes the bridge of the eternal. Whisper inwardly your own words of commitment, or simply breathe and let silence seal it.

This is the oath of embodiment: to no longer separate what you know from how you live. To no longer postpone your wholeness for another day. To live as the embodied truth now, without conditions. The moment you claim this, the circle closes, and the infinite opens.

14.3 Walking as Ceremony

Every step you take can either be unconscious or consecrated. To walk as ceremony means choosing the latter, not by ritual alone, but by remembering that each movement is an offering. The ground beneath you is never just dirt or stone. It is a living field that holds memory, energy, and presence. When you walk with awareness, you weave yourself into that field. You no longer wander through life as a visitor. You become a participant in a sacred dialogue between earth, sky, and spirit.

Walking as ceremony does not require special robes or complex rituals. It begins with intention. When you rise from your bed in the morning and place your feet on the floor, you can declare inwardly, "This step matters. This step is a prayer." That small remembrance shifts the ordinary into the extraordinary. Each pace becomes a heartbeat of devotion. Each stride imprints light into the invisible fabric of reality. The simple act of moving through space transforms into a living transmission of presence.

There is a rhythm to ceremonial walking that is deeper than pace or speed. It is the rhythm of alignment. Your body is upright, your breath steady, your awareness resting in the heart. With every step, you feel the pulse of the earth and allow it to synchronize with your own. You are no longer pushing through life as if trying to get somewhere. You are arriving with every single footfall. Ceremony is not about reaching the end but about sanctifying the path itself.

When walking this way, the veil between worlds thins. The ordinary landscape around you begins to shimmer. A simple street may feel like a temple. The sky may seem to hum with unseen constellations. Even the most mundane surroundings take on a glow, because you are perceiving through the lens of the sacred. This is the shift: you are not waiting for a holy place to appear. You create the holy place with the presence you bring.

Ceremonial walking is also an act of grounding. Many seekers aim for the stars and forget the soil beneath them. Yet the truth of embodiment is that the cosmos and the earth are not two separate realms. They meet in your step. With each foot touching the ground, you affirm your connection to the body of the earth. With each upward lift, you affirm your connection to the infinite above. In this movement, you are the bridge. You are not trapped in the human condition, nor are you lost in the ether. You are the uniting thread of both.

There is also a power in recognizing that each step carries energy forward. What you walk with, you spread. If you walk with resentment, it seeps into the field you pass through. If you walk with reverence, that energy lingers as a blessing for all who come after. Walking as ceremony is an act of stewardship. You are leaving trails of energy behind you, like glowing markings on the earth. These trails are not visible to the eye, yet they shape the atmosphere for those who follow.

The practice is simple but profound. Begin by slowing your pace slightly. Place your awareness in your feet, then in your heart, then in the crown of your head. Feel yourself as a vertical channel between sky and ground. As you move, breathe with intention. Let each inhalation draw in the infinite, and each exhalation bless the path beneath you. Imagine subtle patterns of light imprinting with each step, as if your footprints were glowing symbols laid into the earth. You are walking not only for yourself but as a carrier of frequency.

Walking as ceremony also reshapes how you approach transitions in life. A doorway is no longer just a threshold between rooms. It becomes a veil between worlds. Crossing it consciously turns the ordinary act of entering into a sacred initiation. The same is true when moving from one phase of life into another. By treating each step as ceremonial, you carry the strength of presence into every transition, whether physical, emotional, or spiritual.

This way of walking is not a performance. No one else needs to notice. The power lies in your own inner state. You can practice it while walking alone in nature, through crowded streets, or even across the floor of your home. The setting does not matter. What matters is the choice to be awake in your movement, to infuse it with meaning. This choice rewires your perception of daily life. It teaches you that the sacred is not distant or occasional. It is already woven into each breath and step, waiting to be acknowledged.

There will be days when you forget, when you rush unconsciously from one task to the next. But when you return to the practice, you remember that every step is an entry into presence. The ceremony is never broken. It only waits for you to step back into it. Over time, the act of walking with intention becomes second nature. You no longer force yourself to remember. You embody it as naturally as breathing.

Walking as ceremony is the culmination of living truthfully. It is the lived expression of the oath of embodiment. You are no longer dividing sacred and ordinary, spirit and body, infinite and human. You are all of them, moving as one. Each stride you take ripples outward into the field, unseen yet deeply felt. You become not just a person walking through the world but a living prayer, leaving trails of light behind you. This is the essence of walking as ceremony: to know that every movement is part of a sacred exchange. Your steps bless the earth, and the earth in turn blesses you. You walk through shimmering veils not because they suddenly appeared, but because you finally remembered to see them.

Closing Transmission – You Are the Wisdom Now

There comes a moment when every seeker realizes the search has led them back to themselves. You have walked through spirals, crossed thresholds, carried light into the ordinary, and learned to stand as both receiver and giver. You have touched the silence behind symbols, opened the inner compass, and embodied the truth that what you once longed for is already alive within you.

The truth is simple yet vast: you are no longer just a student of wisdom, you are its living expression. Wisdom is not information you gather, nor teachings you repeat from memory. Wisdom is how you breathe, how you listen, how you show up when no one is watching. It is the way your presence changes a room without words, the way your silence becomes nourishment for others.

The circle is complete, but not closed. Like every spiral, it keeps unfolding, returning you to familiar points but at new heights. Life will test you. People will challenge you. Circumstances will ask if you truly trust what you now carry. Each time, you will remember: I am the wisdom now. It does not belong to a temple, a book, or a teacher. It is the pulse in my chest, the knowing in my bones, the light that cannot be stolen.

The greatest act you can perform is to live this knowing. Live it in how you eat, speak, rest, and love. Live it in how you forgive yourself, in how you see through illusions, in how you refuse to shrink when your presence is needed. Live it by becoming a walking transmission of truth, so that without even trying, you remind others of who they are.

You are the wisdom now. Carry it with humility. Guard it with reverence. Share it with discernment. And above all, embody it fully, because the world does not change when someone talks about wisdom, it changes when someone becomes wisdom.

Bridging to the Bonuses

As you step beyond these pages, there are sacred tools waiting to support your next steps. Think of them as keys placed gently in your hand, practical guides and living practices designed to keep your inner fire steady and bright. They are not add-ons, but living extensions of this transmission. Download them. Work with them. Let them anchor what you've unlocked here so that wisdom doesn't remain a concept, but becomes the rhythm of your days. Because this book was never meant to end, it was meant to begin.

Go to the link below or scan the QR code

bit.ly/bookofwisdombonus

Made in the USA
Columbia, SC
20 December 2025